redefining
life: **FOR WOMEN**

redefining life: **FOR WOMEN**

A NAVSTUDY FEATURING **THEMESSAGE**®//**REMIX**™

Written and compiled by Margaret Feinberg

TH1NK
P.O. Box 35001
Colorado Springs, Colorado 80935

© 2006 by The Navigators

All rights reserved. No part of this publication may be reproduced in any form without written permission from NavPress, P.O. Box 35001, Colorado Springs, CO 80935.

www.navpress.com

TH1NK is an imprint of NavPress.

TH1NK and the TH1NK logo are registered trademarks of NavPress. Absence of ® in connection with marks of NavPress or other parties does not indicate an absence of registration of those marks.

ISBN 1-57683-985-0

Cover design by Kirk DouPonce, DogEaredDesign.com
Cover image by Ranald Mackechnie, Getty
Creative Team: Nicci Hubert, Kathy Mosier, Arvid Wallen, Bob Bubnis

Written and compiled by Margaret Feinberg

All Scripture quotations in this publication are taken from *THE MESSAGE* (MSG). Copyright © 1993, 1994, 1995, 1996, 2000, 2001, 2002. Used by permission of NavPress Publishing Group.

Printed in the United States of America

1 2 3 4 5 6 7 8 9 10 / 10 09 08 07 06

FOR A FREE CATALOG OF
NAVPRESS BOOKS & BIBLE STUDIES,
CALL 1-800-366-7788 (USA)
OR 1-800-839-4769 (CANADA)

contents

About the REDEFININGLIFE Series   7

INTRODUCTION   9

HOW TO USE THIS DISCUSSION GUIDE   11

Lesson 1: FROM GIRL TO WOMAN:
GROWING UP   15

Lesson 2: ON MISSION: LIVING AN
ANCIENT FAITH TODAY   31

Lesson 3: THE TWENTYSOMETHING CRISIS:
WELCOME TO ADULTHOOD   45

Lesson 4: JUST ONE OF THE GIRLS:
BUILDING RICH RELATIONSHIPS   61

Lesson 5: IN SEARCH OF A SOUL MATE:
FINDING MR. RIGHT   75

Lesson 6: MORE THAN SKIN DEEP: COMING
TO TERMS WITH YOUR BODY   91

Lesson 7: TRUE WEALTH: DISCOVERING
SPIRITUAL DISCIPLINES   105

Lesson 8: THE LIFE YOU WERE MEANT FOR:
EMBRACING A WHOLLY HOLY LIFE   119

DISCUSSION GROUP STUDY TIPS	135
FREQUENTLY ASKED QUESTIONS	137
NOTES	141

about the redefininglife series

It's in Christ that we find out who we are and what we are living for.

Ephesians 1:11

For most of your life, you've been a student. And yet in a moment—probably marked by a ceremony—the title you carried for more than a dozen years was stripped away. So now how will you describe yourself when people ask? Are you a professional? An adult? A temporarily unemployed graduate? What seems to fit? Or do any of these fit at all?

Expectations are probably pretty high. But only a few of your graduating class fall into the life you wish you could have—the great job, the wonderful lifelong relationship, the incredible devotion to God. For the rest of you, it's back to square one in many ways. What has been defined for you in the past is suddenly up for negotiation.

The discussion guides in the REDEFINING LIFE series give you a forum to help with that negotiation process. They can help you figure out who you are, *who you really are*, whether you're still taking classes, employed full-time, or somewhere in between. They can help you find out what's really important in life, how to thrive in your work, and how to grow lifelong, meaningful relationships.

REDEFINING LIFE is a place to ask the hard questions of yourself and others. We're talking about a "marrow deep" kind of honesty. At the very least, these discussion guides will show you that you're not alone in the process of self-definition. And hopefully, they will also give you a glimpse—or maybe more—of God's role in the defining of you.

introduction

```
Go out into the world uncorrupted, a breath of
fresh air in this squalid and polluted society.
Provide people with a glimpse of good living and
of the living God.
```

Philippians 2:15

It's not really a choice. You can try to fight it, postpone it, or ignore it, but even without your approval, you are constantly becoming a woman. Hopefully you're in the process of becoming the woman God has called and created you to be: full of life and love and grace and a heart that beats after His own.

If you reflect on the story of Creation found in Genesis 1, you'll discover that God repeatedly saw His work as good until He noted that man was alone. Then, God said for the first time in Scripture, "It's not good." And so He made woman: a beautiful, vibrant creature who reflected His glory.

God has specifically created you as a woman, and He's made no mistake! He's given you a unique blend of gifts, skills, and personality that's specifically designed to honor Him.

This discussion guide will give you a forum to help you reflect and grow as a woman into all the things God has for you. But this kind of journey was not designed to be traveled alone. That's why this series is built around a discussion group where you can safely ask tough questions and be challenged in new ways. In your group you'll learn that you're not alone in the process of becoming the woman God has created you to be. As you journey with the other members of your group, they will help you draw closer to the relationship God desires with you, His daughter.

how to use this discussion guide

REDEFINING LIFE isn't like any other study. We're not kidding. REDEFINING LIFE isn't designed with easy, obvious-to-answer questions and nice fill-in-the-blanks. It's got more of a wide-open-spaces feel to it.

The process is simple, really. Complete a lesson *on your own* (see details below). Then get with your small group and go through it again *together*. Got it?

Okay, want a little more direction than that? Here you go. And if you want even more help, check out the Discussion Group Study Tips (page 135) and the Frequently Asked Questions (page 137) sections in the back of the book.

1. Read, read, read. Each lesson contains five sections, but don't think of them as homework. This isn't an assignment to be graded. And at the end of the week, you don't have to turn it in to a teacher, professor, or boss. So don't read this as a "have to" but as a "get to." Think about how you read when you're on vacation. Set a leisurely pace. Try to enjoy what you read. Then read it again. Allow the words and meaning to soak in. Use the

---

first thoughts

like:

dislike:

agree:

disagree:

don't get it:

---

redefininglife

First Thoughts box to record your initial reactions to the text. (That's a sample on the previous page.) Then use the space provided in and around the reading to make notes. What bugs you? What inspires you? What doesn't make sense? What's confusing? Be honest. Be real. Be yourself. Don't shy away from phrases or sentences you don't understand or don't like. Circle them. Cross them out. Add exclamation marks or smiley faces.

2. Think about what you read. Think about what you wrote. Always ask:

- What does this mean?
- Why does this matter?
- How does this relate to my life right now?
- What does Scripture have to say about this?

Then respond to the questions provided. If you have a knack for asking questions, don't be shy about writing some of your own. You may have a lot to say on one topic, little on another. That's okay. When you come back to the passages in your small group, listen. Allow the experience of others to broaden your understanding and wisdom. You'll be stretched here — called on to evaluate what you've discovered and asked to make practical sense of it. In community, that stretching can often be painful and sometimes even embarrassing. But your willingness to be transparent — your openness to the possibility of personal growth — will reap great rewards. Vulnerability spurs growth in yourself and others.

3. Pray as you go through the entire session — before you begin reading, as you're thinking about a passage and its questions, and especially before you get together in a small group. Pause 'n' pray whenever you need to ask God for help along the way. Prayer takes many forms. You can speak your prayers. Be silent. Write them in the space at the bottom of each page. You can pray a Scripture or a spiritual song. Just don't forget that one of the most important parts of prayer is taking time to listen for God's response.

4. Live. What good are study, reflection, and prayer if they don't lead to action? When reflecting on the week's worth of lessons, think about what impacted you and how you can turn that lesson into action. After studying the issue of forgiveness, you may realize you need to write a letter or email to someone. After studying God's generosity, you may feel compelled to give a gift to a particular outreach. Figure out what God is calling you to do to live out your faith. Sometimes you'll finish a week's worth of lessons and each group member will decide to commit to the same goal. Other times you'll each walk away with a different conviction or goal. Record your goals in the book.

5. Follow up. What good are information and conversation if they don't lead to transformation? Your goal in doing any good study is to ultimately become more like Christ, and this is no exception. Prepare yourself to take your faith and make it active and alive. Be willing to set goals and hold others (as well as be held) accountable in your group. Part of being in a community of Jesus-followers means asking, "Hey, did you do what you said you were going to do?" It will help you put your faith into action as part of a community.

6. Repeat as necessary.

LESSON 1

from girl to woman: growing up

> Don't become so well-adjusted to your culture that you fit into it without even thinking. Instead, fix your attention on God. You'll be changed from the inside out. Readily recognize what he wants from you, and quickly respond to it. Unlike the culture around you, always dragging you down to its level of immaturity, God brings the best out of you, develops well-formed maturity in you.
>
> Romans 12:2

the defining line

We start every lesson by asking you to do a sometimes-difficult thing: define the core truths about the study topic as it relates to you right now. Use this "beginning place" to set the foundation for the lesson. You can then build, change, adjust, and otherwise redefine your life from here.

The truth is that we are all constantly changing, growing, and maturing. With every moment, we age. With every experience, we learn. With every encounter, we discover something new about ourselves.

The journey into womanhood is hard to pin down. It doesn't happen overnight; rather, through a series of rich moments, new experiences, and fresh encounters, we find ourselves making the transition to adulthood.

In the space below, draw a picture of where you see yourself in that transition.

What moments make you feel most like a woman? In what moments do you still feel like a girl?

What do you think makes the difference between being a girl and being a woman?

Consider sharing your responses with your group when you meet.

read Captivating (Part One)

From *Captivating: Unveiling the Mystery of a Woman's Soul* by John and Stasi Eldredge[1]

I'm trying to remember when I first knew in my heart that I was no longer a girl, but had become a woman. Was it when I graduated from high school, or college? Did I know it when I married? When I became a mother? I am forty-five years old as I write this, but there remain places in my heart that feel still so very young. As I think back on what would be considered rites of passage in my life, I understand why my journey has felt so unguided, uncertain. The day I started my period, my family embarrassed me at the dinner table by breaking out in song, "This girl is a woman, now . . ." Hmmmm. I didn't feel any different. All I felt was mortified that they knew. I stared at my plate, suddenly fascinated by corn.

The day I got my first bra, a training bra, the kind with stretchy material over the front, one of my sisters pulled me into the hallway where, to my horror, my father stood at the ready to take my picture. They said I would laugh about it later. (I haven't.) Like so many other women I was left alone to navigate my way through adolescence, through my changing and awakening body, a picture of my changing and awakening heart. No counsel was given for the journey into womanhood. I was encouraged, however, to eat less. My father pulled me aside and told me, "No boy will love you if you're fat."

I joined the feminist movement in college, searching, as so many women did in the '70s, for a sense of self. I actually became director of the Women's Resource Center at a liberal state university in California. But no matter how much I asserted my strength and independence as a woman ("hear me roar"), my heart as a woman remained empty. To be told when you are young and searching that "you can be anything" is not helpful. It's too vast. It gives no direction. To be told when you are older that "you can do anything a man can do" isn't helpful, either. I didn't want to be a man. What does it mean to be a woman?

> **first thoughts**
>
> like:
>
> dislike:
>
> agree:
>
> disagree:
>
> don't get it:

think

- Describe a time when you first felt like a woman. What made it significant?
- Can you identify any of your "rites of passage" of becoming a woman?
- What does it mean "to be a woman" for you? When do you most feel like a woman? When do you most still feel like a girl?
- List three things you love about being a woman. What is the absolute best thing about being a woman?

pray

read Captivating (Part Two)

From *Captivating: Unveiling the Mystery of a Woman's Soul* by John and Stasi Eldredge[2]

I know I am not alone in this nagging sense of failing to measure up, a feeling of not being good enough as a woman. Every woman I've ever met feels it—something deeper than just the sense of failing at what she does. An underlying, gut feeling of failing at who she is. I am not enough, and, I am too much at the same time. Not pretty enough, not thin enough, not kind enough, not gracious enough, not disciplined enough. But too emotional, too needy, too sensitive, too strong, too opinionated, too messy. The result is Shame, the universal companion of women. It haunts us, nipping at our heels, feeding on our deepest fear that we will end up abandoned and alone.

After all, if we were better women—whatever that means—life wouldn't be so hard. Right? We wouldn't have so many struggles; there would be less sorrow in our hearts. Why is it so hard to create meaningful friendships and sustain them? Why do our days seem so unimportant, filled not with romance and adventure but with duties and demands? We feel unseen, even by those who are closest to us. We feel unsought—that no one has the passion or the courage to pursue us, to get past our messiness to find the woman deep inside. And we feel uncertain—uncertain what it even means to be a woman; uncertain what it truly means to be feminine; uncertain if we are or ever will be.

Aware of our deep failings, we pour contempt on our own hearts for wanting more. Oh, we long for intimacy and for

---

first thoughts

like:

dislike:

agree:

disagree:

don't get it:

adventure; we long to be the Beauty of some great story. But the desires set deep in our hearts seem like a luxury, granted only to those women who get their acts together. The message to the rest of us—whether from a driven culture or a driven church—is try harder.

think

- What do you think it means to be feminine? Is being feminine and being a woman the same thing? Explain.
- Why do you think so many women feel like they have to "measure up"? What supports this mind-set in the church? In the workplace? In God?
- Are there any areas in which you feel like you have to "measure up" as a woman? How do you deal with this tendency? In what areas have you made peace with yourself and God?
- Are you more aware of your failings or your successes? Why?

pray

read Rich Relationships

Luke 1:26-38

In the sixth month of Elizabeth's pregnancy, God sent the angel Gabriel to the Galilean village of Nazareth to a virgin engaged to be married to a man descended from David. His name was Joseph, and the virgin's name, Mary. Upon entering, Gabriel greeted her:

> Good morning!
> You're beautiful with God's beauty,
> Beautiful inside and out!
> God be with you.

She was thoroughly shaken, wondering what was behind a greeting like that. But the angel assured her, "Mary, you have nothing to fear. God has a surprise for you: You will become pregnant and give birth to a son and call his name Jesus.

> He will be great,
>> be called 'Son of the Highest.'
> The Lord God will give him
>> the throne of his father David;
> He will rule Jacob's house forever—
>> no end, ever, to his kingdom."

Mary said to the angel, "But how? I've never slept with a man."
The angel answered,

> The Holy Spirit will come upon you,
>> the power of the Highest hover over you;
> Therefore, the child you bring to birth
>> will be called Holy, Son of God.

"And did you know that your cousin Elizabeth conceived a son, old as she is? Everyone called her barren, and here she is six months pregnant! Nothing, you see, is impossible with God."

And Mary said,

> Yes, I see it all now:
> > I'm the Lord's maid, ready to serve.
> Let it be with me
> > just as you say.

Then the angel left her.

---

first thoughts

like:

dislike:

agree:

disagree:

don't get it:

---

think

- In what ways did Mary have to grow up quickly through this encounter?
- What effect do you think this event had on Mary's transition from girl to woman?
- How do you think you would respond if an angel appeared to you and delivered the same message that Mary heard? Does anything surprise you about Mary's response?

- Why do you think God allowed Elizabeth and Mary to be pregnant at the same time? What kind of support do you think the women provided for each other?
- Do you have a supportive person like Elizabeth in your life now? If so, describe.

pray

read Thoughts on Women

From *Present Concerns: A Compelling Collection of Timely, Journalistic Essays* by C. S. Lewis[3]

One of the determining factors in social life is that in general (there are numerous exceptions) men like men better than women like women. Hence, the freer women become, the fewer exclusively male assemblies there are. Most men, if free, retire frequently into the society of their own sex: women, if free, do this less often. In modern social life the sexes are more continuously mixed than they were in earlier periods. This probably has many good results: but it has one bad result. Among young people, obviously, it reduces the amount of serious argument about ideas. When the young male bird is in the presence of the young female it must (Nature insists) display its plumage. Any mixed society thus becomes the scene of wit, banter, persiflage, anecdote—of everything in the world rather than the prolonged and rigorous discussion on ultimate issues, or of those serious masculine friendships in which such discussion arises. Hence, in our student population, a lowering of metaphysical energy. The only serious questions now discussed are those which seem to have a "practical" importance (i.e. the psychological and sociological problems), for these satisfy the intense practicality and concreteness of the female. That is, no doubt, her glory and her proper contribution to the common wisdom of the race.

first thoughts

like:

dislike:

agree:

disagree:

don't get it:

think

- In what ways do you agree or disagree with the statement that "men like men better than women like women"?
- As you've grown older, do you tend to spend more time with male or female friends?
- In what ways are your female friendships more important today than ever?
- In what ways do your girlfriends challenge you to grow that your male friends cannot? How has God used women to bring you closer in your relationship with Him?

pray

read For Such a Time

Esther 2:7-8,17,21-22; 3:8-11,13-14; 4:8-16

The following contains a brief look at the life of Esther, a woman whose bravery was used to save countless lives at a crucial moment in history.

Mordecai had reared his cousin Hadassah, otherwise known as Esther, since she had no father or mother. The girl had a good figure and a beautiful face. After her parents died, Mordecai had adopted her.

When the king's order had been publicly posted, many young girls were brought to the palace complex of Susa and given over to Hegai who was overseer of the women. Esther was among them. . . .

The king fell in love with Esther far more than with any of his other women or any of the other virgins — he was totally smitten by her. He placed a royal crown on her head and made her queen in place of Vashti. . . .

On this day, with Mordecai sitting at the King's Gate, Bigthana and Teresh, two of the king's eunuchs who guarded the entrance, had it in for the king and were making plans to kill King Xerxes. But Mordecai learned of the plot and told Queen Esther, who then told King Xerxes, giving credit to Mordecai. When the thing was investigated and confirmed as true, the two men were hanged on a gallows. This was all written down in a logbook kept for the king's use. . . .

Haman then spoke with King Xerxes: "There is an odd set of people scattered through the provinces of your kingdom who don't fit in. Their customs and ways are different from those of everybody else. Worse, they disregard the king's laws. They're an affront; the king shouldn't put up with them. If it please the king, let orders be given that they be destroyed. I'll pay for it myself. I'll deposit 375 tons of silver in the royal bank to finance the operation."

The king slipped his signet ring from his hand and gave it to Haman son of Hammedatha the Agagite, archenemy of the Jews.

"Go ahead," the king said to Haman. "It's your money — do whatever you want with those people." . . .

Bulletins were sent out by couriers to all the king's provinces with orders to massacre, kill, and eliminate all the Jews — youngsters and old men, women and babies—on a single day, the thirteenth day of the twelfth month, the month Adar, and to plunder their goods. Copies of the bulletin were to be posted in each province, publicly available to all peoples, to get them ready for that day. . . .

Mordecai also gave Hathach, a royal eunuch, a copy of the bulletin that had been posted in Susa ordering the massacre so he could show it to Esther when he reported back with instructions to go to the king and intercede and plead with him for her people.

Hathach came back and told Esther everything Mordecai had said. Esther talked it over with Hathach and then sent him back to Mordecai with this message: "Everyone who works for the king here, and even the people out in the provinces, knows that there is a single fate for every man or woman who approaches the king without being invited: death. The one exception is if the king extends his gold scepter; then he or she may live. And it's been thirty days now since I've been invited to come to the king."

When Hathach told Mordecai what Esther had said, Mordecai sent her this message: "Don't think that just because you live in the king's house you're the one Jew who will get out of this alive. If you persist in staying silent at a time like this, help and deliverance will arrive for the Jews from someplace else; but you and your family will be wiped out. Who knows? Maybe you were made queen for just such a time as this."

Esther sent back her answer to Mordecai: "Go and get all the Jews living in Susa together. Fast for me. Don't eat or drink for three days, either day or night. I and my maids will fast with you. If you will do this, I'll go to the king, even though it's forbidden. If I die, I die."

first thoughts

like:

dislike:

agree:

disagree:

don't get it:

think

- Though the passage doesn't reveal much about Esther's childhood, in what ways do you think Esther had to transition from girl to woman through this experience?
- Why do you think that Esther was willing to risk her life? Do you think you would have been willing to risk your own life in the same situation?
- What kinds of circumstances in your own life have made you grow up fast?
- Have you ever experienced a "for just such a time as this" moment? If so, describe. If not, do you think that such moments still exist today? Explain.

pray

live   The Redefining

Take a few moments to skim through the notes you've made in these readings. What do they tell you about how you view yourself? Your relationship with God? Based on what you've read and discussed, are there any areas where you need to reevaluate how you feel about yourself or your faith?

Do you have any unrealistic expectations about what your life is supposed to look like right now? How are those expectations affecting your view of yourself? Your relationship with others? Your relationship with God? What can you do to replace those views with a healthier perspective of who God has created you to be at this stage in life?

Is anything holding you back?

What can you do in the upcoming months to celebrate the fullness of being God's child?

Talk with a close friend about all of the above. Brainstorm together about what it might take to move toward God in this area of your life. Determine what this looks like in a practical sense and then list any measurable goals you want to shoot for here. Review these goals each week to see how you're doing.

LESSON 2

on mission:
living an ancient faith today

```
Haven't I commanded you? Strength! Courage! Don't
be timid; don't get discouraged. GOD, your God, is
with you every step you take.
```

Joshua 1:9

a reminder

Before you dive into this study, spend a little time reviewing what you wrote in the previous lesson's Live section. How are you doing? Check with your small-group members and review your progress toward the specified goals. If necessary, adjust your goals and plans and then recommit to them.

the defining line

Many followers of Jesus are familiar with the Great Commission. They know that Christ's final command is to go and make disciples. Yet have you ever noticed the promise that accompanies the commission? Jesus says that He will be with you always until the very end. But it's not just a New Testament promise. God's promise to be with His people extends from the beginning of time until the end. That means that the same Jesus who was so real and present and engaged in biblical times is just as real, present, and engaged today. In other words, the faith journey is not dated or ancient but rather is infused with a timeless God today.

In what ways are you tempted to think about your faith as an ancient religion? In what ways do you struggle to connect the teachings of Jesus with modern times? In what ways do you struggle to translate those teachings to others?

In what ways are the teachings of Jesus timeless? Make a list of at least three of His teachings that have transcended time. Discuss them with your group.

Can you think of any teachings from Jesus that don't apply today?

Consider sharing your responses with your group when you meet.

read The Pursuit of God

From *The Pursuit of God* by A. W. Tozer[1]

The moment we make up our minds that we are going on with this determination to exalt God over all, we step out of the world's parade. We shall find ourselves out of adjustment to the ways of the world, and increasingly so as we make progress in the holy way. We shall acquire a new viewpoint; a new and different psychology will be formed within us; a new power will begin to surprise us by its upsurgings and its outgoings.

Our break with the world will be the direct outcome of our changed relation to God. For the world of fallen men does not honor God. Millions call themselves by His name, it is true, and pay some token respect to Him, but a simple test will show how little He is really honored among them. Let the average man be put to the proof on the question of who or what is *above*, and his true position will be exposed. Let him be forced into making a choice between God and money, between God and men, between God and personal ambition, God and self, God and human love, and God will take second place every time. Those other things will be exalted above. However the man may protest, the proof is in the choices he makes day after day throughout his life.

---

first thoughts

like:

dislike:

agree:

disagree:

don't get it:

think

- What defines real faith for Tozer? What's your response to his definition? What defines real faith for you?
- As a woman, do you feel like you're in "the world's parade"? Why or why not? What do you need to do to get out of the parade?
- Do you agree or disagree with the "simple test" described? Who or what would you say is above in your own life right now?
- How do your daily choices affect your faith? What choices are you currently making that are building your faith as a woman? Are you making any choices that are undermining your faith?

pray

read Intimately Known

Jeremiah 1:4-10

This is what God said:

"Before I shaped you in the womb,
    I knew all about you.
Before you saw the light of day,
    I had holy plans for you:
A prophet to the nations—
    that's what I had in mind for you."

But I said, "Hold it, Master God! Look at me.
    I don't know anything. I'm only a boy!"

God told me, "Don't say, 'I'm only a boy.'
    I'll tell you where to go and you'll go there.
I'll tell you what to say and you'll say it.
    Don't be afraid of a soul.
I'll be right there, looking after you."
    God's Decree.

God reached out, touched my mouth, and said,
    "Look! I've just put my words in your mouth—hand-delivered!
See what I've done? I've given you a job to do
    among nations and governments—a red-letter day!
Your job is to pull up and tear down,
    take apart and demolish,
And then start over,
    building and planting."

> **first thoughts**
>
> like:
>
> dislike:
>
> agree:
>
> disagree:
>
> don't get it:

think

- Are there any ways that you feel being a woman affects your ability to respond to God's calling on your life? If so, explain.
- How does being a woman better equip you to fulfill the specific calling you feel God has on your life?
- What insecurities do you have when it comes to following God and responding to His gentle nudges in your life?
- Do you think you have a "job" to do for God? If so, what is it? If not, what are you doing to discover God's plans and purposes for your life?
- Do you think it's your responsibility to uncover God's will or do you think He will naturally make it known? Explain.
- How has God spoken to you or led you in the past? How does this influence the way you expect Him to speak to you or lead you in the future?

pray

read Velvet Elvis

From *Velvet Elvis* by Rob Bell[2]

The very nature of orthodox Christian faith is that we never come to the end. It begs for more. More discussion, more inquiry, more debate, more questions.

It's not so much that the Christian faith *has* a lot of paradoxes. It's that it *is* a lot paradoxes. And we cannot resolve a paradox. We have to let it be what it is.

Being a Christian then is more about celebrating mystery than conquering it.

The Eastern church father Gregory of Nyssa talked about Moses' journey up Mount Sinai in Exodus 19. When Moses enters the darkness toward the top of the mountain, he has moved beyond knowledge to awe and to love and to the mystery of God. Gregory insists that Moses has not arrived when he enters the darkness of the mountaintop. His journey and exploration have only really begun.

Which leads to a really obvious observation: A trampoline only works if you take your feet off the firm, stable ground and jump into the air and let the trampoline propel you upward. Talking about trampolines isn't jumping; it's talking. Two vastly different things. And so we jump and we invite others to jump with us, to live the way of Jesus and see what happens. You don't have to know anything about the springs to pursue living "the way."

In brickworld [the confined world we often find ourselves living in], the focus often becomes getting people to believe the right things so they can be "in." There is often a list of however many doctrines, and the goal is to get people to intellectually assent to these things being true. Once we believe the right things, then we're in. And once we're in, the goal often becomes learning how to get others in with us. I know this is harsh, but in many settings it is true. It is possible in these settings to be, and to believe all of the correct things, and even to be effective at getting others in, and yet our hearts can remain unaffected. It's possible to believe all the right things and be miserable. It's possible to believe all the right doctrines and not live as Jesus teaches us to live. This is why I am so passionate about the trampoline. I want to invite people to actually live this way so the life Jesus offers gradually becomes their life. It becomes less and less about talking, and more and more about the experience we are actually having.

---

first thoughts

like:

dislike:

agree:

disagree:

don't get it:

---

think

- Do you tend to run toward or away from the mysterious nature of God? Do you want to celebrate or conquer the mysteries of the Christian life or Christian faith? Why?
- Are you more tempted to talk about the "trampoline" of faith or to jump up and down? What stops you from inviting more people, including other women, to jump up and down with you and live the way of Jesus?
- How does this passage affect the way you share your faith with others? How does it affect the way you relate to other women?

pray

read Blatantly Honest

From *Searching for God Knows What* by Donald Miller[3]

Last year I caught an interview with Tom Arnold regarding his book *How I Lost Five Pounds in Six Years.* The interviewer asked why he had written the book, and I was somewhat amazed at the honesty of Arnold's answer. The comedian stated that most entertainers are in show business because they are broken people, looking for affirmation. "The reason I wrote this book," Tom Arnold said, "is because I wanted something out there so people would tell me they liked me. It's the reason behind almost everything I do." I have to tell you, after that, I really liked Tom Arnold. Leave it to an ex-alcoholic to tell the truth about life.

A few weeks later I was giving an interview in Seattle when the host asked me the same question of Tom Arnold: "Why did you write this book?" I wondered, on the air, if the explanation Tom Arnold gave was not the same reason I do what I do, and in the end I had to concede my motives of faith often take a backseat to my broken nature and desire to feel validity in life. I told the guy in Seattle that I am broken, that I like to write, but basically, subconsciously, I just want people to like me. The guy in Seattle leaned back in his chair, paused for a moment and said, "You aren't alone."

first thoughts

like:

dislike:

agree:

disagree:

don't get it:

think

- In what ways do you connect with Tom Arnold's quote? If you were in the same situation, do you think you'd answer the question any differently? Why or why not?
- Do you think the core issues that men and women struggle with are more often the same or different? Explain.
- In what ways does your need for affirmation affect your faith as a woman? In what ways does it affect how you communicate your faith with others?
- What role does honesty play in communicating your faith in a modern world?
- Are there any areas where you feel like you need to receive affirmation from God? Explain. What steps do you need to take to make that affirmation real?

pray

read Rebels with a Cause

Daniel 1:1-16

It was the third year of King Jehoiakim's reign in Judah when King Nebuchadnezzar of Babylon declared war on Jerusalem and besieged the city. The Master handed King Jehoiakim of Judah over to him, along with some of the furnishings from the Temple of God. Nebuchadnezzar took king and furnishings to the country of Babylon, the ancient Shinar. He put the furnishings in the sacred treasury.

The king told Ashpenaz, head of the palace staff, to get some Israelites from the royal family and nobility—young men who were healthy and handsome, intelligent and well-educated, good prospects for leadership positions in the government, perfect specimens!—and indoctrinate them in the Babylonian language and the lore of magic and fortunetelling. The king then ordered that they be served from the same menu as the royal table—the best food, the finest wine. After three years of training they would be given positions in the king's court.

Four young men from Judah—Daniel, Hananiah, Mishael, and Azariah—were among those selected. The head of the palace staff gave them Babylonian names: Daniel was named Belteshazzar, Hananiah was named Shadrach, Mishael was named Meshach, Azariah was named Abednego.

But Daniel determined that he would not defile himself by eating the king's food or drinking his wine, so he asked the head of the palace staff to exempt him from the royal diet. The head of the palace staff, by God's grace, liked Daniel, but he warned him, "I'm afraid of what my master the king will do. He is the one who assigned this diet and if he sees that you are not as healthy as the rest, he'll have my head!"

But Daniel appealed to a steward who had been assigned by the head of the palace staff to be in charge of Daniel, Hananiah, Mishael, and Azariah: "Try us out for ten days on a simple diet of vegetables and water. Then compare us with the young men who eat from the royal menu. Make your decision on the basis of what you see."

The steward agreed to do it and fed them vegetables and water for ten days. At the end of the ten days they looked better and more robust than all the others who had been eating from the royal menu. So the steward continued to exempt them from the royal menu of food and drink and served them only vegetables.

---

first thoughts

like:

dislike:

agree:

disagree:

don't get it:

---

think

- In what specific ways do you feel like your faith moves opposite modern culture? How do you respond when modern culture encourages you to do one thing but God encourages you to do another? At what moments do you feel the most torn as a woman?
- How would you have responded if you were in Daniel's situation? Have you faced a similar situation in your school or workplace or home? If so, describe.
- Why is it important to have people in your life who share the same belief system? In what ways do you think Daniel, Hananiah, Mishael, and Azariah were encouraged by going through this experience together? How are your girlfriends currently encouraging you?
- Do you tend to move toward or pull away from other women when you're going through a tough time? Why?

pray

live The Redefining

Take a few moments to skim through the notes you've made in these readings. What do they tell you about your faith right now? Based on what you've read and discussed, is there anything you want to change? Describe this below.

What, if anything, is stopping you from making this change?

Are you allowing anyone or anything to define who you really are and what you really believe? If so, who or what is defining you? What are the results of that in your life? Do you need to make a change?

In what ways do you see your faith being shaped by Christ? In what areas of your life are you living as the world defines you?

Talk with a close friend about all of the above. Brainstorm together about what it might take to move toward God in this area of your life. Determine what this looks like in a practical sense and then list any measurable goals you want to shoot for here. Review these goals each week to see how you're doing.

LESSON 3

the twentysomething crisis: welcome to adulthood

> It feels again that we are leaving who we were, moving on into the people we will become, hopefully, people with some kind of answers, some kind of thing to believe that makes sense of beauty, of romance.
>
> Donald Miller

a reminder

Before you dive into this study, spend a little time reviewing what you wrote in the previous lessons' Live sections. How are you doing? Check with your small-group members and review your progress toward the specified goals. If necessary, adjust your goals and plans and then recommit to them.

the defining line

It's been argued that there's a twentysomething crisis or a quarterlife crisis of sorts taking place in our generation. We're no longer waiting until our forties or fifties to ask tough questions about who we are and what we were created to do. In fact, recent college graduates want more than just a job (though that would be nice); they want a purpose, a sense of belonging, a place where they can use the gifts and talents God has given them. They want to be fulfilled.

But the road to fulfillment—the road God has designed them to travel—is often filled with deeper questions and doubts. You may have struggled with a few of them yourself: Who am I? What's my purpose? What was I created for? Will anyone ever love me? What's real? What's next? Will everything really work out in the end? And how does God fit into all of this?

If you've quietly asked yourself one or more of these questions, you are not alone. In the space below, write down three questions that you quietly ask yourself but are afraid to say out loud.

What prevents you from sharing your struggles and doubts with others?

In what ways does trying to do things on your own limit your ability to grow and experience the fullness of life?

Consider sharing your responses with your group when you meet.

read Inside the Mind of Garden State

Zach Braff, in an interview with *Hatch* magazine, regarding his debut film, *Garden State*[1]

Zach Braff—often found crashing into medical equipment and being called female names by the other doctors on *Scrubs*—exposes a slightly more serious side. At a roundtable on the release of his new movie, Braff talked about his life as a twentysomething and as a newcomer to the directing world. He seems to have an experienced perspective on both.

Did you ever have a quarterlife crisis?
This whole movie's about my quarterlife crisis! I remember thinking when I first heard about the book (*Quarterlife Crisis*, Penguin Putnam, 2001), "Wow, that's an awesome articulation of life as a twentysomething." I'd never heard that before, so I quote it all the time.

So, did you write the movie before you got the part in *Scrubs*?
Yeah, well, particularly from 22 to 28, I'd feel really "in it" as we say in the movie . . . trying to paddle myself above water, I was just feeling really lost and depressed, and I got a big break with *Scrubs* in 2001. The first thing I did was quit my waiting tables job—which, by the way, that conversation in the restaurant was verbatim something that was said to me. So I quit my waiting tables job, and the next day found out we wouldn't be shooting *Scrubs* for four months, and I like to keep busy and thought I would go crazy just sitting and watching TV, so I said, "I gotta write this." Even getting the show didn't really put me out of the depression I was in. So I just sat down and wrote for four months straight, and that was the first draft of *Garden State*. . . .

What keeps you going, chasing your dreams?
Even with a hit show on TV and Natalie Portman signed on, it seemed like every single person in Hollywood was passing on the movie. It was . . . difficult . . . you have to really persevere, a whole lot of doors close in your face. *Scrubs* got me in the door, got the script to the top of the pile, but didn't necessarily sell the movie. But if you believe in what you're making and have

a passion, all you need is access to the right people. It's like being a salesman, enrolling them in your passion.

Movie-making is my real passion, my dream. I went to school to be a film director. I took a detour by taking acting jobs in New York, which I loved doing and made more money than trying to climb the ladder as a PA on a Mariah Carey video.

Do you have a philosophy, a mantra for life?
I once read a quote, I forgot who said it, that life is way too important to take too seriously, and I've always had that taped to my desk, and it always reminds me of how fast life goes and how whenever you start attaching so much meaning to everything and creating all this drama that it was best to strive to laugh it off. And Sam [Portman] wasn't saying she was great at that, she was saying, "Do I cry? Of course I cry. Do I have pain? Of course I have pain. But at the end of the day, I just try and laugh because it's silly to take anything too seriously."

---

first thoughts

like:

dislike:

agree:

disagree:

don't get it:

think

- Did you see the movie *Garden State*? If so, how did you respond to the film? In what ways do you think the movie accurately represents our generation?
- In what ways do you see Braff's philosophy and perspective embraced among your friends? How does his perspective compare with your own?
- How would you define your philosophy of life? Write a description. How are you living out this philosophy each day? How does God fit into that philosophy?

pray

read Not Alone

1 Kings 19:1-10

Ahab reported to Jezebel everything that Elijah had done, including the massacre of the prophets. Jezebel immediately sent a messenger to Elijah with her threat: "The gods will get you for this and I'll get even with you! By this time tomorrow you'll be as dead as any one of those prophets."

When Elijah saw how things were, he ran for dear life to Beersheba, far in the south of Judah. He left his young servant there and then went on into the desert another day's journey. He came to a lone broom bush and collapsed in its shade, wanting in the worst way to be done with it all — to just die: "Enough of this, GOD! Take my life — I'm ready to join my ancestors in the grave!" Exhausted, he fell asleep under the lone broom bush.

Suddenly an angel shook him awake and said, "Get up and eat!"

He looked around and, to his surprise, right by his head were a loaf of bread baked on some coals and a jug of water. He ate the meal and went back to sleep.

The angel of GOD came back, shook him awake again, and said, "Get up and eat some more — you've got a long journey ahead of you."

He got up, ate and drank his fill, and set out. Nourished by that meal, he walked forty days and nights, all the way to the mountain of God, to Horeb. When he got there, he crawled into a cave and went to sleep.

Then the word of GOD came to him: "So Elijah, what are you doing here?"

"I've been working my heart out for the GOD-of-the-Angel-Armies," said Elijah. "The people of Israel have abandoned your covenant, destroyed the places

first thoughts

like:

dislike:

agree:

disagree:

don't get it:

LESSON 3: THE TWENTYSOMETHING CRISIS: WELCOME TO ADULTHOOD

of worship, and murdered your prophets. I'm the only one left, and now they're trying to kill me."

think

- How do you respond to fear? How is your response to fear different than Elijah's response?
- In what ways do you think women experience and express fear differently than men?
- Why do you think Elijah felt that he was the "only one left"? Have you ever felt like you were the only one going through a situation? If so, describe.
- How can isolation hurt the soul of a woman specifically?
- Think of a moment when you found comfort in knowing that you were not the only one going through a situation. Describe how you felt.

pray

read What the Heck Am I Going to Do with My Life?

From *What the Heck Am I Going to Do with My Life? Find Your Place in This World* by Margaret Feinberg[2]

Beth, a 25-year-old, says that when she enrolled in college, she realized it was time to finally answer the question, "What do you want to be when you grow up?" The only problem was that she didn't have an answer.

"I think I put a lot of pressure on myself feeling that my job would be my life's purpose, so I wanted it to be something I really had a passion for and would enjoy doing," she says. "I took a lot of different classes my first few years of college trying to figure it all out. I envied my roommate and others who just knew from the time they were small and were on their way to doing it. I, on the other hand, would spend much time wondering and praying what I would do."

In college, Beth took an Introduction to Social Work class and felt that out of everything she studied, the subject matter was the closest she could come to picking a career once she graduated. "Deep down I think I knew that wasn't the best thing, but it was the best thing at the time," she says.

She graduated with a degree in social work and worked in the field for a few years. "I loved the work and the children I worked with and felt like when I went home and laid my head down at night, I had spent the day doing something worthwhile to society and purposeful. But I became burned out from working way too many hours in very stressful situations and realized that I could not continue the pace and demands that social work required for the rest of my life."

Beth began to wonder what else she could do with her life. "There I was again, wondering what in the world I wanted to be and do and a bit frustrated again to be in that place. I began fervently praying and seeking God's direction and knew that even though I had no idea, He had formed and made me and knew the answers I was searching for. So I prayed and waited."

In the meantime, she quit her job and moved home with her parents to rest and de-stress for a month. She continued praying and began substitute teaching to pay the bills. "(God) began to put the field of nursing on my heart," she recalls. "I looked into it, and I am now completing my first semester of nursing school. I'm starting over, wondering what in the heck I'm doing in nursing school but feeling a remarkable peace."

Beth says she has come to terms with the fact that life is too complex to figure it all out. "I wish someone had told me when I was in school the first time that it was okay if I didn't know. At that age it is kind of hard to know what you want to do with the rest of your life. I really had to go out into the world and get some life into me before I really could see and know what all is out there to be and do. I think I put way too much pressure on myself and didn't enjoy the process of not knowing and discovering what I liked and might be good at doing."

I can identify all too well with the stress and pressure Beth describes. Figuring out what to do with your life isn't easy, because even after landing a job or finally earning a few years' work experience to put on the résumé, the questions about what you are going to do don't always disappear. They just keep resurfacing. Singles, newlyweds, oldlyweds, emptynesters, retirees—anyone in any age or stage in life—can wrestle with these questions and struggle to find answers. No one is immune.

That's one reason why I think *what the heck am I going to do with my life?* is one of the greatest questions we will ever ask ourselves. Not just because it is the question that won't go away, but because it forces us to examine ourselves in a new light—who we are today and who we are called to be tomorrow. The question challenges us to look at the core of who we are as individuals, discover our talents and giftings, and come to terms with our weaknesses. When we dare to ask the question, *what the heck am I going to do with my life?*, we step into a realm where anything—including growth, transformation and change—is possible. Risk, failure and loss are all potential outcomes, but so are success, innovation and the possibility of building a legacy that lives beyond us.

What the heck am I going to do with my life? isn't a safe question, but it has the power to awaken dormant dreams and silent desires. It has the ability to both compel and propel us to fulfill our lifelong calling and purpose. And that makes it a question worth asking.

> **first thoughts**
>
> like:
>
> dislike:
>
> agree:
>
> disagree:
>
> don't get it:

think

- When was the last time you asked yourself, "What the heck am I going to do with my life?" How would you respond to that question today?
- Have you ever pursued a profession, career, or area of study only to discover it wasn't a good fit? How did you respond?
- Do you think it's possible to discover what you're created to do without doing some things that you're not created to do? Do you think it's possible to discover who you really are without going through challenging times? Why or why not?
- What's been the biggest surprise about adulthood? What piece of advice would you give to someone else entering the real world?

pray

LESSON 3: THE TWENTYSOMETHING CRISIS: WELCOME TO ADULTHOOD

read Great Expectations

Genesis 37:3-8,12-14,18-28

Israel loved Joseph more than any of his other sons because he was the child of his old age. And he made him an elaborately embroidered coat. When his brothers realized that their father loved him more than them, they grew to hate him—they wouldn't even speak to him.

Joseph had a dream. When he told it to his brothers, they hated him even more. He said, "Listen to this dream I had. We were all out in the field gathering bundles of wheat. All of a sudden my bundle stood straight up and your bundles circled around it and bowed down to mine."

His brothers said, "So! You're going to rule us? You're going to boss us around?" And they hated him more than ever because of his dreams and the way he talked. . . .

His brothers had gone off to Shechem where they were pasturing their father's flocks. Israel said to Joseph, "Your brothers are with flocks in Shechem. Come, I want to send you to them."

Joseph said, "I'm ready."

He said, "Go and see how your brothers and the flocks are doing and bring me back a report." He sent him off from the valley of Hebron to Shechem. . . .

They spotted him off in the distance. By the time he got to them they had cooked up a plot to kill him. The brothers were saying, "Here comes that dreamer. Let's kill him and throw him into one of these old cisterns; we can say that a vicious animal ate him up. We'll see what his dreams amount to."

Reuben heard the brothers talking and intervened to save him, "We're not going to kill him. No murder. Go ahead and throw him in this cistern out here in the wild, but don't hurt him." Reuben planned to go back later and get him out and take him back to his father.

When Joseph reached his brothers, they ripped off the fancy coat he was wearing, grabbed him, and threw him into a cistern. The cistern was dry; there wasn't any water in it.

Then they sat down to eat their supper. Looking up, they saw a caravan of Ishmaelites on their way from Gilead, their camels loaded with spices, ointments, and perfumes to sell in Egypt. Judah said, "Brothers, what are we going to get out of killing our brother and concealing the evidence? Let's sell him to the Ishmaelites, but let's not kill him—he is, after all, our brother, our own flesh and blood." His brothers agreed.

By that time the Midianite traders were passing by. His brothers pulled Joseph out of the cistern and sold him for twenty pieces of silver to the Ishmaelites who took Joseph with them down to Egypt.

---

first thoughts

like:

dislike:

agree:

disagree:

don't get it:

---

think

- In what ways has your life turned out like you expected? Is there anything that has really surprised you or thrown you for a loop?
- When things don't turn out like you expect, who are you most likely to blame? Yourself? Someone else? God? Why?
- Think of a time when you thought you heard from God. What confirmed it for you? What made you question?
- Describe a time when you can look back and see that God was at work even in the middle of a difficult time.

pray

LESSON 3: THE TWENTYSOMETHING CRISIS: WELCOME TO ADULTHOOD

read Paradise Lost

From *Quarterlife Crisis: The Unique Challenges of Life in Your Twenties* by Alexandra Robbins and Abby Wilner[3]

All of these factors—intense self-doubt, problems with learning a new work or social protocol, being overwhelmed by everything happening at once, losing the college anchor, dashed expectations—can contribute to a sense of helplessness that many twentysomethings feel in the years after graduation. Several twentysomethings told us the best way to describe this feeling is to say they feel lost, hopeless and clueless which can trigger or prolong a precarious emotional period. "After graduation, I didn't have any real plans," says Sandra, a 25-year-old in Birmingham, Alabama. "I figured I would just go home and live in the town I grew up in, and the thought depressed me. In fact, I got so upset that I started crying nonstop—I mean, literally, I couldn't stop crying."

---

first thoughts

like:

dislike:

agree:

disagree:

don't get it:

---

think

- How is our generation different than previous generations? How do you think the struggles that we face as young women are different than what our moms faced?

redefininglife

- Have you gone through any periods of self-doubt or feeling overwhelmed or hopeless while transitioning to the real world? If so, explain.
- Does this passage help you develop any compassion for other women who may be struggling with post-graduation blues? Explain.
- In what ways have you made happiness a priority in your life? What makes you truly happy? In what ways do the things that make you happy honor God? How much of your time and energy is spent on those things?

pray

LESSON 3: THE TWENTYSOMETHING CRISIS: WELCOME TO ADULTHOOD

live The Redefining

Take a few moments to skim through the notes you've made in these readings. In what ways do you think you've experienced a twentysomething or quarterlife crisis? In what areas do you think you're still experiencing one? Describe below.

What are some of the deeper questions you're wrestling with currently in your life? Where are you turning for answers?

After reflecting on this chapter, are there any changes you want to make in your life? What, if anything, is stopping you from making those changes?

Why do you think it's so important to know that you're not alone when you're facing a difficult issue, such as the quarterlife crisis? What can you do to help build a healthy network of friends in your life?

Talk with your small group about all of the above. Ask everyone in the group to make a list of prayer requests based on the personal challenges in their lives. Make copies of the prayer requests for everyone and commit to praying for all the members of your group. Each week check back with group members to see how God is responding.

LESSON 4

just one of the girls: building rich relationships

> By yourself you're unprotected.
> With a friend you can face the worst.
> Can you round up a third?
> A three-stranded rope isn't easily snapped.
>
> Ecclesiastes 4:12

a reminder

Before you dive into this study, spend a little time reviewing what you wrote in the previous lessons' Live sections. How are you doing? Check with your small-group members and review your progress toward the specified goals. If necessary, adjust your goals and plans and then recommit to them.

the defining line

Friends are one of God's richest treasures. A good friend will encourage you when you're down, challenge you when you're heading in the wrong direction, and laugh with you during life's funniest moments. Learning to build, develop, and nurture your relationship with other women will add depth, texture, and richness to your life.

redefininglife

Take a few moments to reflect on some of your best girlfriends. What traits do they have in common? Make a list below.

What is the most important quality to you in a friend? What do you think is the most important quality you offer in a friendship?

What are some of the lessons you've learned from your girlfriends? What have they taught you about Jesus?

Share your responses with the others in your group. Think about how the members of your group complement one another.

read The Making of a Friend

From "Friendship" by Bill Saxman[1]

So what makes a friend? In all the world, I think I have four friends and I consider myself very rich. As I remember, Jesus only used the term friend twice. Once when he told the disciples that he no longer called them servants but friends and the other when Judas came to betray him with a kiss and Jesus said, "Friend, do what you are here to do." To be a friend is to be in a relationship that is only exceeded by the love of family. What makes a friend? Friendship begins with trust, a willingness to be you, warts and all. Friends reciprocate, not in terms of one-up-manship but on the basis of care. A friend not only knows what you are doing but why you are doing it. A friend may not agree with you, may even strongly disagree but the relationship you have is not threatened. As one person said, "Friends are those for whom I would swing over hell on a rotten rope." With friends there is heart communication. With friends you are able to pick up the threads of life, no matter when they are dropped. Friendship does not die; acquaintances pass through the night, and neighbors move but friends are forever. The song that opened an old radio show almost had it correct, "Friendship, friendship, what a perfect blendship, when other friendships have been forgot, theirs will still be hot." The truth is that friends are experienced, not described.

first thoughts

like:

dislike:

agree:

disagree:

don't get it:

think

- How would you define the word *friend* in your own life? How is a friend different than an acquaintance or neighbor?
- How long does it take you to make friends? Would you describe the process of making a friend easy or difficult for you? What is required for you to consider someone a friend?
- In what ways do you agree with the statement, "Friends are experienced, not described"? In what ways do you disagree?
- Reflecting on your closest girlfriends, how did the relationships start? Do you see any patterns in the way God causes your life to intersect with others?

pray

read Soul Sisters

From "Soul Sisters" by Jane Rubietta[2]

God created us for deep, authentic, sustaining relationships—for soul friendships. A soul friend will connect deeply with you in matters of the heart and soul. This friend has permission to ask hard questions: "How's your marriage going? How are you growing closer to God in this trying situation?" This friend covenants to hear your past without condemnation, hold your dreams for the future carefully, and wait with you in the present.

A soul friend goes beyond a Bible study or prayer partner, though Scripture and prayer are part of what you share. Deep soul friends commit to push you toward integrity when you're on the verge of fragmenting.

I've been in a covenant group with five other women for eight years. We have covenanted to journey together and to push one another closer to Christ. They nail me when they see me speaking one thing and living another. "You are in danger of becoming spiritually schizophrenic," they said to me once.

Knowing my writing and speaking frequently focus on rest and finding quiet places with God, they saw a disconnect between my soul and my lifestyle. I was speaking a lot (sometimes 15 times a month), writing furiously, and trying to be a wife and mother. My heart was splitting, and they refused to passively watch the fragmentation continue.

A friend who knows your spirit has your number! She can provide stability and offer accountability. A soul friend goes deeper by learning your dreams and hopes, whether specific, like the dream to write I once shared hesitatingly in a group, or broader hopes, like becoming a person God could use however He chooses. A soul friend offers accountability even in unspoken areas.

Suzie will call out what she believes is in my heart, even though I'm not living it at the moment. "I know you really want to be this kind of a woman, Jane, though you may not see it right now," she might say, reminding me where I want to head.

A soul friend sees past your messiness—the places where you blow it, the relationships that haven't worked, and the mistakes you've made. She loves you in spite of yourself and is committed for the long haul.

> **first thoughts**
>
> like:
>
> dislike:
>
> agree:
>
> disagree:
>
> don't get it:

think

- Make a list of the "soul friends" in your life right now, both far and near. Now make a list of the ways they've enriched your life.
- Is there anything that prevents you from going deeper in your relationship with your girlfriends? If so, explain.
- What can you do to become a better friend to another woman?
- List three women in your life right now who make you want to be more like Jesus. Now make a list of three women you are challenging and loving so they can become more like Jesus.

pray

read Upright Relationships

Romans 12:9-21

Love from the center of who you are; don't fake it. Run for dear life from evil; hold on for dear life to good. Be good friends who love deeply; practice playing second fiddle.

Don't burn out; keep yourselves fueled and aflame. Be alert servants of the Master, cheerfully expectant. Don't quit in hard times; pray all the harder. Help needy Christians; be inventive in hospitality.

Bless your enemies; no cursing under your breath. Laugh with your happy friends when they're happy; share tears when they're down. Get along with each other; don't be stuck-up. Make friends with nobodies; don't be the great somebody.

Don't hit back; discover beauty in everyone. If you've got it in you, get along with everybody. Don't insist on getting even; that's not for you to do. "I'll do the judging," says God. "I'll take care of it."

Our Scriptures tell us that if you see your enemy hungry, go buy that person lunch, or if he's thirsty, get him a drink. Your generosity will surprise him with goodness. Don't let evil get the best of you; get the best of evil by doing good.

---

first thoughts

like:

dislike:

agree:

disagree:

don't get it:

think

- Can you think of any people you struggle to get along with? What wisdom does this passage offer in how to improve those relationships?
- Have you ever encountered someone you didn't like at first but over time became a close friend with? Describe your experience. What made the difference?
- What changes do you need to make in your attitude and actions in order to "discover beauty in everyone"?
- How can you "love from the center of who you are"?
- Is there anyone you consider your enemy? How do you avoid cursing under your breath and choose instead to bless that person?

pray

read The Blessing of Friendship

Ruth 1:3-19

Elimelech died and Naomi was left, she and her two sons. The sons took Moabite wives; the name of the first was Orpah, the second Ruth. They lived there in Moab for the next ten years. But then the two brothers, Mahlon and Kilion, died. Now the woman was left without either her young men or her husband.

One day she got herself together, she and her two daughters-in-law, to leave the country of Moab and set out for home; she had heard that GOD had been pleased to visit his people and give them food. And so she started out from the place she had been living, she and her two daughters-in-law with her, on the road back to the land of Judah.

After a short while on the road, Naomi told her two daughters-in-law, "Go back. Go home and live with your mothers. And may GOD treat you as graciously as you treated your deceased husbands and me. May GOD give each of you a new home and a new husband!" She kissed them and they cried openly.

They said, "No, we're going on with you to your people."

But Naomi was firm: "Go back, my dear daughters. Why would you come with me? Do you suppose I still have sons in my womb who can become your future husbands? Go back, dear daughters—on your way, please! I'm too old to get a husband. Why, even if I said, 'There's still hope!' and this very night got a man and had sons, can you imagine being satisfied to wait until they were grown? Would you wait that long to get married again? No, dear daughters; this is a bitter pill for me to swallow—more bitter for me than for you. GOD has dealt me a hard blow."

Again they cried openly. Orpah kissed her mother-in-law good-bye; but Ruth embraced her and held on.

Naomi said, "Look, your sister-in-law is going back home to live with her own people and gods; go with her."

But Ruth said, "Don't force me to leave you; don't make me go home. Where you go, I go; and where you live, I'll live. Your people are my people, your God is my god; where you die, I'll die, and that's where I'll be buried, so help me GOD—not even death itself is going to come between us!"

When Naomi saw that Ruth had her heart set on going with her, she gave in. And so the two of them traveled on together to Bethlehem.

---

first thoughts

like:

dislike:

agree:

disagree:

don't get it:

---

think

- Ruth and Naomi were brought together under rather unusual circumstances. How have you met some of your closest friends? How can the ways you've made friends in the past make you more sensitive to the ways God may be introducing new women into your life in the future?
- Do you think true friendship always contains an element of choice? Explain why or why not.
- In what ways do you put expectations on your friends that they cannot possibly fulfill?

pray

read Tell It Like It Is

From "Tell It Like It Is: How to Speak the Truth to a Friend Without Harming Your Friendship" by Annette Smith[3]

I'll always remember when my good friend, Sheri, called me on the carpet about my attitude problem. I'm thankful now, but at the time . . .

Sheri and I were sitting in her cozy kitchen sipping coffee and nibbling on bake-sale leftovers. "I saw Darla in Sears yesterday," she said. "She's lost a bunch of weight."

"Wonder how long it'll take her to gain it back this time," I said, reaching for a *third* macadamia nut cookie. "She always does, you know."

Darla-of-the-fluctuating-weight and I once had been good friends. Not any more. For more than a year, we'd barely spoken. Even though Darla had made numerous attempts to mend the rift in our relationship, one caused by a misunderstanding involving our children, I continued to nurse a grudge against her.

"Darla told me her eldest daughter just got accepted into medical school," said Sheri. "Her middle girl's engaged to an attorney, and her son's in line to be awarded the high school's art scholarship this year."

"Darla always thinks her kids are better than anyone else's," I sniffed.

After refilling my mug, Sheri looked me in the eye and said, "Annette, we need to talk. Hasn't it been long enough? What's the deal with you *still* having such a hateful attitude toward Darla? Everyone who knows you can tell you don't like her."

"It's that obvious?"

"It is. And Annette, listen to me." My friend put her hand on my arm. "Whatever the problem is, you need to get over it. Your attitude isn't right, and you know it."

Ouch. Sheri's honest words hurt my feelings. But they also affected me in a way a dozen sermons on forgiveness hadn't. She was absolutely right. My hateful attitude was wrong. We talked some more, and I was overcome with shame and remorse. That night I prayed for forgiveness for myself and for blessings for Darla and her family.

Later that week, with shaking hands and a pounding heart, I delivered homemade banana nut bread and a ribbon-wrapped cinnamon candle to Darla's new house. That afternoon, over glasses of iced tea, Darla and I spoke careful words of apology and forgiveness. We avoided the specifics of what had caused our estrangement; it seemed pointless to visit that place again. What mattered to us both was our mutual desire to make things right.

Today, Darla and I are real friends again, thanks to Sheri's honest words.

first thoughts

like:

dislike:

agree:

disagree:

don't get it:

think

- Why do you think it's so hard for women to speak the truth in love? What prevents you from speaking the truth in love more often?
- Think of a time when you confronted a girlfriend about an issue. How did you approach the issue? What was the response? Is there anything you wish you would have done differently?
- Think of a time when someone confronted you about an issue. How did you respond? What did you learn from it?
- Is there anyone in your life now you've been meaning to address about an issue? What's stopping you from having that conversation?

pray

live   The Redefining

Take a few moments to skim through the notes you've made in these readings. What do they tell you about your relationship with other women? Based on what you've read and discussed, are there any changes that you want to make in your relationship with them? Are there any issues that you need to sit down and discuss with anyone in particular? Describe this below.

What, if anything, is stopping you from making those changes or having the discussion with that person?

Are you allowing anything to stop you from being a better friend? Are there any changes you need to make in your attitude, behavior, or schedule?

What can you do to be a better friend to the people God has placed in your life? Are there any long-lost friends you need to track down?

Talk with your group about all of the above. Brainstorm together about what it might take to strengthen your friendships. Determine what this looks like in a practical sense and then list any measurable goals you want to shoot for here. Review these goals each week to see how you're doing.

LESSON 5

in search of a soul mate: finding mr. right

> Oh, let me warn you, sisters in Jerusalem,
>   by the gazelles, yes, by all the wild deer:
> Don't excite love, don't stir it up,
>   until the time is ripe—and you're ready.
>
> Song of Songs 3:5

a reminder

Before you dive into this study, spend a little time reviewing what you wrote in the previous lessons' Live sections. How are you doing? Check with your small-group members and review your progress toward the specified goals. If necessary, adjust your goals and plans and then recommit to them.

the defining line

It's exciting to think of spending the rest of your life with a godly man you've fallen head over heels in love with! There's the anticipation and a bubbling joy that comes with thinking about your wedding day and the rich years of marriage that will follow.

But if you haven't found "the one" yet, you're probably in a period of waiting and wondering. What will he look like and be like? When will God bring him into your life?

In the space below, explain what the term *soul mate* means to you. Do you think the concept is biblical? Why or why not?

What responsibility do you feel as a woman to search for or pursue "the one"? What responsibility do you think he has to search for or pursue you?

What are you actively doing today to prepare yourself for "the one" God has for you?

Consider sharing your responses with your group when you meet.

read Can Men and Women Be Just Friends?

From "Can Men and Women Be Just Friends?" by Les and Leslie Parrott[1]

For many people, the idea of a man and a woman being friends is charming but improbable. "It always leads to something else," they argue, meaning the relationship eventually becomes romantic or soon fizzles out. Perhaps they are right. After all, in contrast to the countless love stories we see in the movies, male-female friendships are rarely acclaimed or depicted as an ongoing, freestanding bond. How many stories can you think of that richly portray or endorse the lasting, devoted friendship of a man and a woman as an end in itself? Even the acclaimed film *When Harry Met Sally*, which got a lot of people talking about cross-gender friendships, ultimately proved to be another tale of romantic love. Billy Crystal and Meg Ryan's tumultuous and endearing friendship is only a stage in the development of the more celebrated attachment of falling in love.

On the other hand, there are those who are surprised by the question and argue that of course male-female friendships are possible; why wouldn't they be? These people's persuasiveness almost makes the romantic pull of such relationships seem unusual. They seem to ignore romantic possibilities in these friendships altogether. "One of my best friends is a woman," the male proponent of this perspective insists. "And it's never crossed my mind to consider her in a romantic way." Well, that takes care of that. "My friendships with men are far less complex than my friendships with women," a female with this position might say. "My guy friends and I can play sports and just have fun."

In our informal survey of people who are "just friends" with someone of the opposite sex, we heard a number of positive remarks, mostly stemming from the unique way God wired men and women. Over and over, men spoke about how a woman's friendship provided them with a level of nurturing not generally available in their relationships with men. They said things such as, "I don't have to play the macho game with women. I can show my weaknesses to a female friend and she'll still accept me." When we asked women about their friendships with men, we heard comments such as, "He is a good sounding board for getting the male perspective, the kind I can't get from my women friends."

Interestingly, women do not report the same level of intimacy as men do with their cross-gender friendships. Even women who count men among their close friends feel barriers between them. Women will say things such as, "I have fun with men, and they can even be supportive and helpful about some things, but it's just not the same. If I try to talk to my male friends the same way I talk to my female friends, I'm always disappointed." At first glance the payoff for men seems to be bigger than the payoff for women in cross-gender friendships, but that's not necessarily true. Women report great enjoyment from the diversity their friendships with men bring to their lives.

So, does all this mean the answer to the question about men and women being friends is yes? Few relationship issues are that plain and simple. The real answer is "it depends." So, you say, *let's cut to the chase: What do these relationships depend upon?* They depend upon how much each person in the relationship is willing to stretch and grow. These friendships, you see, require both men and women to call upon parts of themselves that are usually less accessible when relating to their typical same-sex friends. For a man, a female friend allows him to express his more emotional side, to experience his vulnerability, to treat himself and his friend more tenderly than is permissible with male friends. What is typically missing for him in this cross-gender relationship, however, is the kind of rough camaraderie he can have with another man. For a woman, friendship with a man helps her express her independent, more reasoned, and tougher side—the harder edge that's kept under wraps in relationships with women. The downside for her is the relative absence of emotional reciprocity and intensity she normally shares with a female friend.

So, okay, twist our arms for a *yes* or *no* answer to this question and the answer will be *yes*. But we

first thoughts

like:

dislike:

agree:

disagree:

don't get it:

will quickly qualify it: Men and women can enjoy friendship together, but not at the same level they do with friends of the same sex.

think

- Based on your own experience, do you think men and women can be just friends? Why or why not? How far can a friendship travel without a "DTR" (Define the Relationship) talk?
- How does your faith affect your relationship with guys? How does it affect the way you interact with guys?
- What can you do to develop stronger and healthier relationships with guys? What can you do to help other women develop stronger and healthier relationships?

pray

read Simplicity

1 Corinthians 7:29-35

I do want to point out, friends, that time is of the essence. There is no time to waste, so don't complicate your lives unnecessarily. Keep it simple—in marriage, grief, joy, whatever. Even in ordinary things—your daily routines of shopping, and so on. Deal as sparingly as possible with the things the world thrusts on you. This world as you see it is on its way out.

I want you to live as free of complications as possible. When you're unmarried, you're free to concentrate on simply pleasing the Master. Marriage involves you in all the nuts and bolts of domestic life and in wanting to please your spouse, leading to so many more demands on your attention. The time and energy that married people spend on caring for and nurturing each other, the unmarried can spend in becoming whole and holy instruments of God. I'm trying to be helpful and make it as easy as possible for you, not make things harder. All I want is for you to be able to develop a way of life in which you can spend plenty of time together with the Master without a lot of distractions.

---

first thoughts

like:

dislike:

agree:

disagree:

don't get it:

---

redefininglife

think

- How do you think our culture views singleness? How is this different from the way the Bible views it?
- What are some of the biggest joys of being a single woman? What do you think you'll miss about being single when you're married?
- What are you doing in your life right now to "keep it simple"? What steps can you take to simplify your work, your relationships, and your daily routines?

pray

read Red-Hot Love

Song of Songs 8:6-7

Love is invincible facing danger and death.
    Passion laughs at the terrors of hell.
The fire of love stops at nothing—
    it sweeps everything before it.
Flood waters can't drown love,
    torrents of rain can't put it out.
Love can't be bought, love can't be sold—
    It's not to be found in the marketplace.

---

first thoughts

like:

dislike:

agree:

disagree:

don't get it:

---

think

- How would you define true love? How would you define romantic love? What is the difference?
- How can you know when you're truly in love?
- What are you looking for in Mr. Right? How has your idea of Mr. Right changed over the last three years?

- Make a list of expectations you have for your future husband. Are any of them unfair or too big for him?

pray

read The Six-Letter Word

Ephesians 5:22-28

Wives, understand and support your husbands in ways that show your support for Christ. The husband provides leadership to his wife the way Christ does to his church, not by domineering but by cherishing. So just as the church submits to Christ as he exercises such leadership, wives should likewise submit to their husbands.

Husbands, go all out in your love for your wives, exactly as Christ did for the church—a love marked by giving, not getting. Christ's love makes the church whole. His words evoke her beauty. Everything he does and says is designed to bring the best out of her, dressing her in dazzling white silk, radiant with holiness. And that is how husbands ought to love their wives. They're really doing themselves a favor—since they're already "one" in marriage.

---

first thoughts

like:

dislike:

agree:

disagree:

don't get it:

---

think

- What does the word *submit* mean to you? What does it mean in the context of this passage?

- Why do you think some women struggle with the word *submit*? Why do you think this language is used in this passage?
- Within this passage, what challenges are listed for husbands? Does anything surprise you about those challenges?
- Why do you think God expresses His love for the church and humanity through the metaphor of marriage? What does it reveal about Him?

pray

read Modern Chastity

Lauren Winner in an interview with Gene Edward Veith of *WORLD* magazine[2]

WORLD: How do you define chastity?

WINNER: As the church has always defined it—all Christians are called to recognize that God created sex for marriage, which means, for married people, chastity = fidelity, only having sex with your spouse, and for unmarried people it means not having sex at all.

Chastity is not just about keeping your pants zipped. It is about renouncing bodily union with another person so that you can find a deeper union with the Body of Christ. This is why some of the recent books on modesty irk me. Many of these books suggest to women that they should be chaste because godly men don't want to date women who wear tubetops; because farmers won't buy the cow if they can get the milk for free; because chaste women will attract godly men. If that's your reason for dressing modestly—if your attention is still focused on attracting the right kind of guy—then I'm not sure you're really inhabiting chastity.

WORLD: How can churches do a better job of teaching about sex?

WINNER: One thing we need to do is give a richer, more theologically robust account of chastity. It's not enough to say "Paul says don't fornicate." . . . Rather, he is seeking to preserve, restore, and protect God's vision for humanity and sexuality, laid out at the opening of Genesis.

WORLD: How can the church become more of a community that can help Christians live chastely?

WINNER: One of the fundamental lies Christians have absorbed from our surrounding individualistic society is that "what I do with my body is none of your concern." Paul instructs the Galatians to hold one another accountable for sin: "Brothers, if someone is caught in a sin, you who are spiritual should restore him gently. . . . Carry each other's burdens." That verse, if we construe it uncharitably, can lead us to envision a community that functions primarily as a police force [but] the more important task of the community is to make sense of the ethical codes that are being enforced. Here the community is not so much cop as storyteller, sustaining the stories that make sense of the community's norms. This storytelling is part of the working out of God's grace in the Church. We do this every time we read Scripture, and every time we celebrate the Lord's Supper, and (hopefully) each time we minister to one another.

---

first thoughts

like:

dislike:

agree:

disagree:

don't get it:

---

think

- How would you define chastity? How have your past experiences shaped your definition?
- In what ways is sexuality a community concern?
- On a scale of 1 to 10, how hard is it for you to be chaste? What kinds of situations make it easier to be chaste? What kinds of situations make it more difficult?
- At what point in a relationship do you establish sexual boundaries? How negotiable are those boundaries as the relationship progresses? What do you think is the purpose of boundaries?

- What can Christians do to encourage a more healthy discussion of sexuality? Are there any topics that should remain off-limits? Explain.

pray

live   The Redefining

Take a few moments to skim through the notes you've made in these readings. What do they reveal about your relationships with guys? Do you tend to have more healthy or unhealthy relationships? Based on what you've read and discussed, is there anything you want to change? Describe this below.

What, if anything, is stopping you from making this change?

In what ways is your perspective on dating, relationships, and sex being shaped by the culture you live in? In what ways is it being shaped by a God-centered perspective?

What steps can you take to have a healthier perspective?

Are there any sexual boundaries that you need to draw in your current romantic relationship? Are there any boundaries you need to establish before you get involved in another relationship? What steps can you take to maintain your boundaries as the relationship progresses?

Talk with a close friend about all of the above. Brainstorm together about what it might take to move toward God in this area of your life. Determine what this looks like in a practical sense and then list any measurable goals you want to shoot for here. Review these goals each week to see how you're doing.

LESSON 6

more than skin deep: coming to terms with your body

Love the Lord your God with all your passion and prayer and muscle and intelligence—and . . . your neighbor as well as you do yourself.

Luke 10:27

a reminder
Before you dive into this study, spend a little time reviewing what you wrote in the previous lessons' Live sections. How are you doing? Check with your small-group members and review your progress toward the specified goals. If necessary, adjust your goals and plans and then recommit to them.

the defining line
Loving God is meant to be holistic. You don't just love Him with your spirit or soul or mind but also with your body—the very fibers of your being. Yet this is a challenge in a society that places such a heavy emphasis on appearance and body shape.

First Corinthians 3:16 says, "You realize, don't you, that you are the temple of God, and God himself is present in you?" But at what point do we find ourselves worshiping the temple rather than God?

On a scale of 1 to 10, how comfortable would you say you feel in your own skin? Using the same scale, how did you feel about yourself five years ago? How do you hope to feel about yourself five years from now?

If you could change one thing about your body, what would it be?

List five things you like about your body.

Now, looking at the previous two questions, which part of your body do you tend to spend your time and energy focused on? What steps can you take to change this focus?

Consider sharing your responses with your group when you meet.

read Finding Fault

From "Finding Fault" by Carin Gorrell[1]

Do magazine editors encourage eating disorders among young women? Perhaps. The majority of women portrayed in magazines as having the "perfect" body type are also extra ordinarily thin, making it easy for society to blame the media for our nation's epidemic of anorexia and bulimia.

Recognizing this dichotomy, researchers are faced with a challenging question: Are magazines to blame for promoting the thin ideal or are their readers—consumers who are responsible for the financial success of magazines?

"The more we know, the less we know," says Steven Thomsen, Ph.D., an associate communications professor at Brigham Young University. "That's the most frustrating part." Thomsen recently completed a study examining the frequency with which eating disordered female high school students read health and fitness magazines—a form of media that should abet healthy lifestyles. His findings, published in the American Journal of Health Education, are both enlightening and disturbing.

Among the nearly 500 students he surveyed, Thomsen found abundant evidence of unhealthy weight control practices in the previous year. Eleven percent of the participants reported that they had used laxatives, 15 percent had taken diet pills, 9 percent induced vomiting and 52 percent said they had restricted their caloric intake to under 1,200 calories per day.

Thomsen then asked the participants how often they read health and fitness, beauty and fashion magazines. He discovered that women who read health and fitness magazines frequently—at least once a month—were also significantly more likely to have practiced unhealthy weight control methods than were moderate or infrequent readers. Nearly 80 percent of frequent readers had induced vomiting, 73 percent had taken diet pills and 60 percent had used laxatives. And nearly two times as many women who limited their daily caloric intake also read health and fitness magazines more frequently compared with those who did not.

Surprisingly, Thomsen also uncovered similar results when examining how frequently eating disorder sufferers read beauty and fashion magazines — neither of which focus on living healthfully. The only difference he did find was among laxative users, who did not frequently read beauty and fashion magazines.

Despite his findings — and his having teenage daughters of his own — Thomsen doesn't blame the media for the prevalence of eating disorders in America. And neither did the study's participants.

"This supports our perception that these magazines may be more of a perpetuating factor than a causal factor," Thomsen says. "It seems that young women who already have eating disordered attitudes and thoughts are turning to the publications for support."

---

first thoughts

like:

dislike:

agree:

disagree:

don't get it:

---

think

- In what ways do you think the media promotes unhealthy and unrealistic expectations about our bodies? In what ways do you feel pressure to conform to the "thin ideal"?
- Have you used unhealthy methods to control your weight? Do you still? If not, what helped you break out of those unhealthy methods?

- Are there still unhealthy methods that you're tempted to use to control your weight? Explain.
- How does your faith affect the way you look at your body?

pray

read Hunger for God

1 Corinthians 6:13-20

You know the old saying, "First you eat to live, and then you live to eat"? Well, it may be true that the body is only a temporary thing, but that's no excuse for stuffing your body with food, or indulging it with sex. Since the Master honors you with a body, honor him with your body!

God honored the Master's body by raising it from the grave. He'll treat yours with the same resurrection power. Until that time, remember that your bodies are created with the same dignity as the Master's body. You wouldn't take the Master's body off to a whorehouse, would you? I should hope not.

There's more to sex than mere skin on skin. Sex is as much spiritual mystery as physical fact. As written in Scripture, "The two become one." Since we want to become spiritually one with the Master, we must not pursue the kind of sex that avoids commitment and intimacy, leaving us more lonely than ever — the kind of sex that can never "become one." There is a sense in which sexual sins are different from all others. In sexual sin we violate the sacredness of our own bodies, these bodies that were made for God-given and God-modeled love, for "becoming one" with another. Or didn't you realize that your body is a sacred place, the place of the Holy Spirit? Don't you see that you can't live however you please, squandering what God paid such a high price for? The physical part of you is not some piece of property belonging to the spiritual part of you. God owns the whole works. So let people see God in and through your body.

first thoughts

like:

dislike:

agree:

disagree:

don't get it:

redefininglife

think

- What are your three favorite foods? Reflecting on your diet, would you honestly say that you "eat to live" or "live to eat"?
- Why do you think food is such a powerful force in our society? Do you think food is more powerful than, less powerful than, or equally as powerful as our culture's emphasis on sex?
- Why do you think this passage makes the connection between indulging in food and indulging in sex? Do you think there's a difference between them in God's eyes? Why or why not?
- What does it mean to "let people see God in and through your body"? How does that affect how you eat? How you behave? What you wear?

pray

read The Thin Cage

From *Life Inside the "Thin" Cage: A Personal Look into the Hidden World of the Chronic Dieter* by Constance Rhodes[2]

Let me tell you about my life inside the thin cage. It is a dark place with little food, little social interaction, and little freedom. Everything is off-limits. Everything is based on performance. If I don't perform well or look good, then I am not good. I am not allowed to enjoy a piece of cake or a slice of pizza because if I do, tomorrow I will wake up fat. I don't get much social interaction because I scare off any would-be friends out of my fear of letting them get too close to me. I exist on water and a few carefully planned meals every day. And coffee—lots of coffee. And Diet Coke, of course. . . .

Daily I complain to my long-suffering husband. . . . "My butt is bigger today, isn't it?" "My stomach didn't look like this last month, did it?" "Are you sure I'm not fat?" "I feel so gross. . . . How can you love me?" It's a wonder he does, but he does.

I'm grouchy all the time and am constantly aware of my cruel nature toward people I wish I could be nicer to.

Since everything is about performance and appearance, a bad hair day can truly ruin me. If my performance ever slips, I am suddenly in the precarious position of losing my value to the world. Going anywhere and meeting anyone requires that I look my best, for people may not like me if they don't think I'm attractive and thin. I have a hard time sleeping at night.

More than anything, I am alone. . . .

---

first thoughts

like:

dislike:

agree:

disagree:

don't get it:

think

- Have you ever felt like you've been inside the "thin cage"? What does your "thin cage" look like? What have you done to break out of it?
- In what ways do performance and appearance go together?
- If someone asks you, "Is my butt too big?" what is the best response?
- Do you struggle with perfectionism? In what ways? How does it affect your attitude toward your body? Your relationships with others? Your relationship with God?

pray

read A Healthy Perspective

Romans 14:13-23

Forget about deciding what's right for each other. Here's what you need to be concerned about: that you don't get in the way of someone else, making life more difficult than it already is. I'm convinced—Jesus convinced me!—that everything as it is in itself is holy. We, of course, by the way we treat it or talk about it, can contaminate it.

If you confuse others by making a big issue over what they eat or don't eat, you're no longer a companion with them in love, are you? These, remember, are persons for whom Christ died. Would you risk sending them to hell over an item in their diet? Don't you dare let a piece of God-blessed food become an occasion of soul-poisoning!

God's kingdom isn't a matter of what you put in your stomach, for goodness' sake. It's what God does with your life as he sets it right, puts it together, and completes it with joy. Your task is to single-mindedly serve Christ. Do that and you'll kill two birds with one stone: pleasing the God above you and proving your worth to the people around you.

So let's agree to use all our energy in getting along with each other. Help others with encouraging words; don't drag them down by finding fault. You're certainly not going to permit an argument over what is served or not served at supper to wreck God's work among you, are you? I said it before and I'll say it again: All food is good, but it can turn bad if you use it badly, if you use it to trip others up and send them sprawling. When you sit down to a meal, your primary concern should not be to feed your own face but to share the life of Jesus. So be sensitive and courteous to the others who are eating. Don't eat or say or do things that might interfere with the free exchange of love.

Cultivate your own relationship with God, but don't impose it on others. You're fortunate if your behavior and your belief are coherent. But if you're not sure, if you notice that you are acting in ways inconsistent with what you believe—some days trying to impose your opinions on others, other days just trying to please them—then you know that you're out of line. If the way you live isn't consistent with what you believe, then it's wrong.

> **first thoughts**
>
> like:
>
> dislike:
>
> agree:
>
> disagree:
>
> don't get it:

think

- Has caring for your body ever become an obsession? Explain. When did things get out of hand?
- Do you think having a thin body is God's priority for your life? Explain.
- Think of a time when you were tempted to comment on another person's diet or eating habits. How did you handle the situation? How did you respond?
- In what ways has the manner in which you feed and care for your body affected your friendships?

pray

read Addicted to Stress

From "Are You Addicted to Stress?" by Lisa Collier Cool[3]

Women have always taken on lots of stress, so why is the dependence on it a new phenomenon? There's a restlessness in our society that's mistaken for normalcy, says Frederic Luskin, coauthor of *Stress Free for Good* and director of Stanford University's Forgiveness Project. Women feel the need to keep up — to constantly be crossing tasks off their to-do lists, to have their cell phones with them at all times, to always be planning the next home project, the next dinner party, the next play date. . . .

The truth is, no one actually thrives on stress: It's supposed to be a short-term reflex; extended bouts of stress take a toll on your emotional and physical health. Being too revved up to relax can make unhealthy habits, like smoking or drinking, seem like a tempting way to slow down. Or after a day of non-stop demands, a woman may forage in the fridge for food — a pattern that Pamela Peeke, M.D., author of *Body for Life for Women*, calls "stew and chew." "When women are stressed, they ruminate, or 'stew' about the hassles in their lives," Peeke explains. "And then they calm themselves by 'chewing,' curling up with a carton of ice cream and blanking everything else out. Besides not helping you get past what's bothering you, this calorie-rich habit can lead to weight gain, which often creates more stress and puts you at risk for diabetes and heart disease. Women also often seek relief through another kind of consumption: They hit the mall."

first thoughts

like:

dislike:

agree:

disagree:

don't get it:

think

- Why do you think there's such a tendency for women to do too much?
- Do you think stress is addictive? Why or why not?
- Have you ever been addicted to stress? Explain.
- On a scale of 1 to 10, how much stress do you have in your life right now? What steps can you take to reduce the amount of stress in your life?
- How do you personally respond to stress? How is that response affecting your overall physical well-being?

pray

live   The Redefining

Take a few moments to skim through the notes you've made in these readings. What do they tell you about your overall health? In what ways does your faith affect the way you care for your body? Are there any areas in which you feel God is nudging you to take better care of yourself? Describe this below.

What, if anything, is stopping you from making this change?

Do you think you have a healthy appreciation for the body God has given you? Do you think you're ever too hard on yourself? What steps can you take to develop a healthier perspective?

What can you do to live a more balanced life? Are there any behaviors you need to change? Are there any activities you need to cut back? Are there any unhealthy emotional or physical situations you need to step away from?

Talk with a close friend about all of the above. Brainstorm together about what it might take to move toward God in this area of your life. Determine what this looks like in a practical sense and then list any measurable goals you want to shoot for here. Review these goals each week to see how you're doing.

LESSON 7

true wealth: discovering spiritual disciplines

"Call to me and I will answer you. I'll tell you marvelous and wondrous things that you could never figure out on your own."

Jeremiah 33:3

a reminder
Before you dive into this study, spend a little time reviewing what you wrote in the previous lessons' Live sections. How are you doing? Check with your small-group members and review your progress toward the specified goals. If necessary, adjust your goals and plans and then recommit to them.

the defining line
God longs for a deeper relationship with you. Even when you don't feel it, you can rest assured that God is passionately pursuing you. But it's not a one-way relationship. God also invites us to pursue Him. He invites you to call after Him and to seek Him. He promises that He will make Himself known.

One of the ways we can pursue God is through spiritual disciplines. When we choose to pray or worship or fast, we are intentionally setting aside our agendas in order to pursue God's. No matter how many or how few years you've been a follower of Jesus, spiritual disciplines can add texture and depth to your relationship with God and help you grow as a believer.

In the space below, make a list of spiritual disciplines that you practice frequently (such as prayer, fasting, studying Scripture, worship, and so on). Which come easier for you as a woman? Which are more difficult?

What growth have you noticed in your life through practicing spiritual disciplines? What prevents you from doing them more often?

Consider sharing your responses with your group when you meet.

read Disciplines of Grace

From *Disciplines of Grace: From Spiritual Routines to Spiritual Renewal* by T. M. Moore[1]

Both routines and disciplines are important in our lives. Yet they are clearly not the same. A problem arises when we allow what are intended to be disciplines to become mere routines—like my summer workouts. When that happens, not only do our disciplines not produce the desired results, but they become tedious, boring and dull. We may be faithful in attending to them, but not in the way they were designed and certainly without much in the way of results to show for our effort.

This problem is especially serious in the area of our spiritual lives when our practice of the disciplines of grace is allowed to become a mere spiritual routine instead.

God has given us the disciplines of grace as means to help us grow in love for him and our neighbors. These precious tools—prayer, the Word of God, worship, solitude, giving, fasting, silence in God's presence and so forth—bring us into his presence in ways that everyday living does not, enabling us to glimpse his glory and tap into his power for daily renewal in Christ. But when our practice of the disciplines of grace is allowed to lapse into routine devotional activities—when our disciplines become mere routines—they lose their power to bring us face to face with the Lord in life-transforming ways.

first thoughts

like:

dislike:

agree:

disagree:

don't get it:

think

- What spiritual disciplines are part of your life? Prayer? Reading the Bible? Worship? Solitude? Social justice? Giving? Silence? Fasting? Worship? What else? How do these disciplines affect your relationship with God?
- Do you think some spiritual disciplines are more natural for women than men? Explain.
- Have you ever had a spiritual discipline become simply a part of your routine? If so, describe.
- What makes the difference between a discipline and a routine? Are there any benefits to routines?
- Are there any spiritual disciplines you've never tried before? What's stopping you from trying them?

pray

read The Discipline of the Sabbath

From "Learning to Exhale: Embrace the Gift of True Sabbath Rest and Gain a New Outlook on Life" by Margaret Feinberg[2]

The idea of Sabbath rest wasn't completely unfamiliar. I had memorized the Ten Commandments in Sunday School and earned a gold sticky star for the accomplishment. But this one was easy to overlook.

Do not murder. Check.

Do not steal. Check.

Do not covet. Check (as best I can).

But when it came to honoring the Sabbath, I reasoned its importance away, as if it were an old, strange law tucked into the Old Testament that didn't really apply today.

What I discovered is it seems to apply today more than ever. Our lives are busy—too busy—as we fill our waking moments with activity. God asks us to put the breaks on our schedule so that we can rest our souls, reorder our worlds, and realign ourselves with Him.

It's no secret that when God created our world in six days he took the seventh to rest. And it wasn't because He was tired. God was demonstrating the importance of restoration to all of creation.

Then keeping the Sabbath showed up as No. 4 in the list of Ten Commandments: "Remember to dedicate the Sabbath day: You are to labor six days and do all your work, but the seventh day is a Sabbath to the Lord your God. You must not do any work.... For the Lord made the heavens and the earth, the sea, and everything in them in six days; then He rested on the seventh. Therefore the Lord

---

first thoughts

like:

dislike:

agree:

disagree:

don't get it:

blessed the Sabbath day and declared it holy" (Exodus 20:8-11).

Scripture is filled with Sabbath references, but one particular passage in the New Testament showed me that it needed more than just lip service in my life. Hebrews 4:9-10 says, "A Sabbath rest remains, therefore, for God's people. For the person who has entered His rest has rested from his own works, just as God did from his."

As I read and re-read that passage, it became a balm on my weary soul. I realized that my physical pain was echoing a message God had been trying to teach me: Enough is enough — you were not designed to work all the time.

think

- How have you made honoring the Sabbath part of your faith journey? What does it mean to you to "take a Sabbath"? What prevents you from taking a Sabbath every week?
- Why do you think rest is such an important discipline in Christianity? Do you think this is a spiritual discipline that comes easier for certain sexes or personality types? Explain. How does rest affect your relationship with God? With others?
- Do you think you work too much or too little? Why?
- Is it possible to live the best possible life without honoring the Sabbath? Explain.
- What steps can you take to embrace the idea of Sabbath as a lifestyle?

pray

read The Discipline of Contentment

Philippians 4:11-13

Actually, I don't have a sense of needing anything personally. I've learned by now to be quite content whatever my circumstances. I'm just as happy with little as with much, with much as with little. I've found the recipe for being happy whether full or hungry, hands full or hands empty. Whatever I have, wherever I am, I can make it through anything in the One who makes me who I am.

Proverbs 30:7-9

And then he prayed, "God, I'm asking for two things
    before I die; don't refuse me—
Banish lies from my lips
    and liars from my presence.
Give me enough food to live on,
    neither too much nor too little.
If I'm too full, I might get independent,
    saying, 'God? Who needs him?'
If I'm poor, I might steal
    and dishonor the name of my God."

---

first thoughts

like:

dislike:

agree:

disagree:

don't get it:

think

- In what ways do you think contentment is a spiritual discipline? Do you think contentment is something that needs to be cultivated among women? Why or why not?
- What do you think prevents people from being more content? Are there areas (such as body image) where contentment is more of a challenge for women? Explain.
- On a scale of 1 to 10, how content are you right now? What prevents you from being more content?
- What steps can you take to become more content right where you are? What can you do to help others become more content?

pray

read The Discipline of Prayer

From *Authentic Faith: The Power of a Fire-Tested Life* by Gary L. Thomas[3]

Waiting also plays a particularly important role for those who want to advance in prayer. Every reputable teacher of prayer I've read has warned that if you truly want to push forward in intimacy with God, you will invariably have to overcome some degree of boredom. It is not realistic to expect that you can fill your mind with endless diversion, static and noise for twenty or thirty years, and then suddenly stop and pray for hours in rapturous delight.

Jeanne Guyon, who wrote a book on prayer in the latter part of the seventeenth century that eventually inspired the likes of John Wesley, François Fénelon, and Hudson Taylor, wrote, "If you set forth the spiritual lands . . . you must realize that times of dryness await you." Guyon warns that in times of prayer dryness, we may be tempted to respond with an abundance of action. She urges a far different response: "You must await the return of your Beloved with patient love." This is because, typically, the action is simply a way to end the boredom; it is not pure action, in that its ultimate end is not to serve God but to spare ourselves the pain of boredom. God sees through this ruse, and thus may ask us to wait for a long time.

first thoughts

like:

dislike:

agree:

disagree:

don't get it:

think

- Is prayer something that comes naturally for you, or is it something you struggle to do?
- How do you deal with "dryness" or "boredom" that can come with extended times of prayer?
- What environments are most likely to make you desire to pray? What prevents you from spending more time in those environments or from waiting for an answer from God? What prevents you from praying more?
- What steps can you take to strengthen or build your prayer and waiting life over the next two weeks? How can you encourage other women to do the same?

pray

read The Discipline of Fasting

Isaiah 58:5-7

"Do you think this is the kind of fast day I'm after:
   a day to show off humility?
To put on a pious long face
   and parade around solemnly in black?
Do you call *that* fasting,
   a fast day that I, GOD, would like?

"This is the kind of fast day I'm after:
   to break the chains of injustice,
   get rid of exploitation in the workplace,
   free the oppressed,
   cancel debts.
What I'm interested in seeing you do is:
   sharing your food with the hungry,
   inviting the homeless poor into your homes,
   putting clothes on the shivering ill-clad,
   being available to your own families."

first thoughts

like:

dislike:

agree:

disagree:

don't get it:

redefining life

think

- Have you ever practiced the spiritual discipline of fasting? If so, describe. If not, what has prevented you from learning more about it?
- What is the purpose of fasting? What other Scriptures can you think of that speak to this issue?
- Why is motivation so important for someone who is fasting? Do you think women are ever tempted to fast for the wrong reasons? Explain.
- How is God honored through fasting? How do you think fasting affects your relationship with God?

pray

LESSON 7: TRUE WEALTH: DISCOVERING SPIRITUAL DISCIPLINES

live The Redefining

Take a few moments to skim through the notes you've made in these readings. What do they reveal about your interactions with God? Based on what you've read and discussed, is there anything you want to change about how you approach your faith? Are there any spiritual disciplines you want to develop in your own life? Describe this below.

What, if anything, is stopping you from making this change?

Do you have any fears or insecurities that prevent you from digging deeper in your relationship with God? In the following space, make a list. Share at least one with the members of your group.

How much pressure do you put on yourself to try to do things on your own? How quick are you to rely on God when difficulties arise? What steps can you take to develop a more even-keeled relationship with God?

Talk with a close friend about all of the above. Brainstorm together about what it might take to move toward God in this area of your life. Determine what this looks like in a practical sense and then list any measurable goals you want to shoot for here. Review these goals each week to see how you're doing.

LESSON 8

the life you were meant for: embracing a wholly holy life

> I will sing for joy in God,
>   explode in praise from deep in my soul!
> He dressed me up in a suit of salvation,
>   he outfitted me in a robe of righteousness,
> As a bridegroom who puts on a tuxedo
>   and a bride a jeweled tiara.
> For as the earth bursts with spring wildflowers,
>   and as a garden cascades with blossoms,
> So the Master, God, brings righteousness into
>   full bloom
>   and puts praise on display before the nations.
>
>   Isaiah 61:10-11

a reminder

Before you dive into this study, spend a little time reviewing what you wrote in the previous lessons' Live sections. How are you doing? Check with your small-group members and review your progress toward the specified goals. If necessary, adjust your goals and plans and then recommit to them.

the defining line

By its very nature, being clothed in Christ makes you beautiful. As God takes up residence in your heart, you can't help but find His presence bursting out from within you and transforming your actions and attitudes.

You were designed to live a God-infused life—but have you taken time to reflect on what that means and how it's shaping you?

In the space below, write a paragraph describing the difference you've seen God make in your life over the last three years. How has knowing God affected you on a personal level?

At what moments do you sense His presence bursting out from within you? When is God most real to you?

Consider sharing your responses with your group when you meet.

read Ruined

From "Ruined" by Brian Orme[1]

In many ways, I think God is anxiously waiting for our weaknesses to emerge so His power can penetrate our safe attempts at Christianity. Revealing your weakness is not safe, but following Jesus was never meant to be safe, in fact, following Jesus will probably ruin your life, in a good way. What will it ruin? It will ruin your ability to keep pretending; it will tear down your ability to live in this world without caring for it, and it will utterly ruin your chances of living out your days as a fugitive hiding from grace.

There's great pain in getting kicked out of the garden and having our sin exposed, but there is also a side of grace that says, "This is for your good." For Adam and Eve, the angel guarding the garden was fierce, but it was also a protector from what could be. The same thing happens over and over again every day; God "exposes" us for the greater good — to protect us from a darker future and preserve us for redemption.

first thoughts

like:

dislike:

agree:

disagree:

don't get it:

think

- In what ways do you feel like you have to keep up the appearances of your faith?
- How do efforts to keep up appearances affect the ability of others to grow spiritually? For you to grow spiritually?
- Do you tend to run toward or away from your weaknesses? Why?
- What prevents you from facing your weaknesses head-on? What prevents you from encouraging other women to face their weaknesses head-on?

pray

read Radiant Love

1 John 3:14-17

The way we know we've been transferred from death to life is that we love our brothers and sisters. Anyone who doesn't love is as good as dead. Anyone who hates a brother or sister is a murderer, and you know very well that eternal life and murder don't go together.

This is how we've come to understand and experience love: Christ sacrificed his life for us. This is why we ought to live sacrificially for our fellow believers, and not just be out for ourselves. If you see some brother or sister in need and have the means to do something about it but turn a cold shoulder and do nothing, what happens to God's love? It disappears. And you made it disappear.

---

first thoughts

like:

dislike:

agree:

disagree:

don't get it:

---

think

- Why do you think God is so concerned with grace, mercy, love, and generosity?
- How do you decide whether it's your responsibility to respond to the need of a fellow follower of Jesus? Have you ever responded

to a need and regretted it? Have you ever responded to a need and seen God work marvelously?

- What does it mean to "live sacrificially" in our abundant culture? Beyond money, what can you sacrifice to make a difference in the lives of others?

pray

read How to Live

Micah 6:8

But he's already made it plain how to live, what to do,
    what GOD is looking for in men and women.
It's quite simple: Do what is fair and just to your neighbor,
    be compassionate and loyal in your love,
And don't take yourself too seriously—
    take God seriously.

James 1:26-27

Anyone who sets himself up as "religious" by talking a good game is self-deceived. This kind of religion is hot air and only hot air. Real religion, the kind that passes muster before God the Father, is this: Reach out to the homeless and loveless in their plight, and guard against corruption from the godless world.

---

first thoughts

like:

dislike:

agree:

disagree:

don't get it:

think

- How would you define "real religion"? What kinds of religious beliefs appear to be "real religion" but are not? Are there any particular areas where women are more susceptible?
- When are you most tempted to "take yourself too seriously"? Are there any things you need to let go of?
- In what ways is Christianity simple? In what ways are you tempted to make it more complex than it is?
- Are there any areas in which you need to be more proactive in guarding against corruption "from the godless world"?

pray

read Every Thought Captive

From *Every Thought Captive: Battling the Toxic Beliefs That Separate Us from the Life We Crave* by Jerusha Clark[2]

Do your thoughts ever seem overwhelming—uncontrollable, untamable, and completely ungodly, despite your best efforts to live righteously? Sometimes I'll review the thoughts I've had over the course of a day, even the course of an hour, and I'll despair: the mean things I've thought about others or myself, the impure, angry, or fearful thoughts that have assaulted me and reminded me how truly fallen I am. If these thoughts were displayed on my forehead for all to see, I'm sure I would live as a hermit.

You may be thinking, *Great . . . What if I'll never be able to conquer the thoughts that pass through my mind? What if someone finds out what I'm really thinking about?*

There's nothing easy about asking yourself these questions, but you're in good compay; every other woman on the face of the earth deals with the same thing. We all struggle with our thought lives, even if we don't know it. And talking with each other honestly about our thought lives rarely happens because it's vulnerable and uncomfortably close. Yet as I've matured, and as I've worked with other women, I've found that evaluating my thoughts, especially in the context of community, is *extraordinarily* important. What I think determines how I feel, which then impacts how I behave.

You may wonder what the big deal is. Perhaps you have no idea what's really going on in your mind because you haven't paid much attention. You think about whatever you want to think about and find it difficult to believe that your thoughts have much of an influence on your behavior, at least not directly. But consider Proverbs 4:23, which reads,

> Be very careful about what you think.
> Your thoughts run your life. (NCV)

Every act, whether beautiful or heinous, starts in the mind. Every charitable act begins with a loving thought, and every sin grows out of a distorted thought. We sin, in large part, because we hold on to and live out of toxic beliefs. So whether we are aware of the depths and brokenness of our thoughts or not, they are very real, and they influence us more than we even know.

Many of our thoughts, unfortunately, are both negative and untrue. At different points in their lives, most women have believed poisonous lies such as these: *I'm not good enough. What others think about me defines who I am. I am the sum of my accomplishments and my relationships.* We have believed a multitude of other self-defeating falsities as well, lies that have hijacked and poisoned our minds.

Joyce Meyer writes, "Thinking about what you're thinking about is very valuable because Satan usually deceives people into thinking that the source of their misery or trouble is something other than what it really is."[3] The Enemy wants us to believe that what we do is more important than what goes on inside us. But our behavior is only a symptom of a deeper problem.

Wouldn't it be wonderful if we could get to the real root of our problems? . . . First Peter 1:13,15 encourages us, "Roll up your sleeves, put your mind in gear . . . let yourselves be pulled into a way of life shaped by God's life, a life energetic and blazing with holiness" (MSG). A life and mind energetic and blazing with holiness — I think deep down that's what we all crave.

---

first thoughts

like:

dislike:

agree:

disagree:

don't get it:

think

- Take a moment to review the thoughts you've had today. How would you describe them? How are they affecting your perspective, outlook, and impact on others—especially other women?
- Are the majority of thoughts you think each day Christ-centered or centered around something else? What can you do to have a more God-infused thought life?
- Reflect on three of the negative thoughts you've had today. Rewrite the same thoughts as you believe God would want you to think them.

pray

read True Faith

Hebrews 11:1-3,8-16

The fundamental fact of existence is that this trust in God, this faith, is the firm foundation under everything that makes life worth living. It's our handle on what we can't see. The act of faith is what distinguished our ancestors, set them above the crowd.

By faith, we see the world called into existence by God's word, what we see created by what we don't see. . . .

By an act of faith, Abraham said yes to God's call to travel to an unknown place that would become his home. When he left he had no idea where he was going. By an act of faith he lived in the country promised him, lived as a stranger camping in tents. Isaac and Jacob did the same, living under the same promise. Abraham did it by keeping his eye on an unseen city with real, eternal foundations — the City designed and built by God.

By faith, barren Sarah was able to become pregnant, old woman as she was at the time, because she believed the One who made a promise would do what he said. That's how it happened that from one man's dead and shriveled loins there are now people numbering into the millions.

Each one of these people of faith died not yet having in hand what was promised, but still believing. How did they do it? They saw it way off in the distance, waved their greeting, and accepted the fact that they were transients in this world. People who live this way make it plain that they are looking for their true home. If they were homesick for the old country,

> **first thoughts**
>
> like:
>
> dislike:
>
> agree:
>
> disagree:
>
> don't get it:

they could have gone back any time they wanted. But they were after a far better country than that—*heaven* country. You can see why God is so proud of them, and has a City waiting for them.

think

- At what moments in the past month have you felt like you've been living according to faith?
- What does it feel like to live by faith? How would you describe it to someone who is unfamiliar with the Bible?
- In what situations are you the most tempted to doubt God? In what situations are you most likely to believe Him?
- What experiences have caused your faith to grow the most?

pray

live   The Redefining

Take a few moments to skim through the notes you've made in these readings. What do they tell you about your relationship with God? Based on what you've read and discussed, are there any areas in which you want to change or grow? Describe them below.

What, if anything, is stopping you from making these changes?

Is there anything in your life — unforgiveness, sin, jealousy, anger — that is preventing you from going deeper in your relationship with God? If so, spend some time this week talking to God about this.

What are you doing to build authentic community, including healthy friendships, in your life? How could you be more intentional about your relationships?

Talk with a close friend about all of the above. Brainstorm together about what it might take to move toward God in this area of your life. Determine what this looks like in a practical sense and then list any measurable goals you want to shoot for here.

Even though you've reached the end of this discussion guide, progress toward building healthy relationships in all areas of your life should continue. Commit to discussing your goals and discoveries with small-group members or friends as you attempt to live a God-infused life every day.

And don't stop here. This is only the beginning of the redefining process. It will last a lifetime. By examining these many different areas of your faith life, you've begun an internal (and eternal) dialogue about who you are and who God created you to be. You're not only a woman; you're His precious child. Reflect on what you've uncovered and keep wrestling with the things you don't quite understand. Come back to this book often to remind yourself of the big goals you've set and the specific ideas you have for reaching them. Take a moment to pray as well, asking God to congeal some of these thoughts into wisdom that will guide the rest of your life.

discussion group
study tips

After going through the study on your own, it's time to sit down with others and go deeper. A group of eight to ten is optimal, but smaller groups will allow members to participate more.

Here are a few thoughts on how to make the most of your group discussion time.

Set ground rules. You don't need many. Here are two:

First, you'll want group members to make a commitment to the entire eight-week study. A binding legal document with notarized signatures and commitments written in blood probably isn't necessary — but *you* know your friends best. Just remember this: Significant personal growth happens when group members spend enough time together to really get to know each other. Hit-and-miss attendance rarely allows this to occur.

Second, agree together that everyone's story is important. Time is a valuable commodity, so if you have only an hour to spend together, do your best to give each person ample time to express concerns, pass along insights, and generally feel like a participating member of the group. Small-group discussions are not monologues.

Meet regularly. Choose a time and place and stick to it. No one likes showing up to a restaurant at noon, only to discover that the meeting was moved to seven in the evening at so-and-so's house. Consistency removes stress that could otherwise frustrate discussion and subsequent personal growth. It's only eight weeks. You can do this.

Think ahead. Whoever is leading or organizing the study needs to keep an eye on the calendar. No matter what day or time you pick, you're probably going to run into a date that just doesn't work for people. Maybe it's a holiday.

Maybe there's a huge concert or conference in town. Maybe there's a random week when everyone is going to be out of town. Keep in communication with each other about the meetings and be flexible if you do have to reschedule a meeting or skip a week.

Talk openly. If you enter this study with shields up, you're probably not alone. And you're not a "bad person" for your hesitation to unpack your life in front of friends or strangers. Maybe you're skeptical about the value of revealing the deepest parts of who you are to others. Maybe you're simply too afraid of what might fall out of the suitcase. You don't have to go to a place where you're uncomfortable. If you want to sit and listen, offer a few thoughts, or even express a surface level of your own pain, go ahead. But don't neglect what brings you to this place—that desperation. You can't ignore it away. Dip your feet in the water of brutally honest discussion and you may choose to dive in. There is healing here.

Stay on task. Be wary of sharing material that falls into the Too Much Information (TMI) category. Don't spill unnecessary stuff. This is about discovering how *you* can be a better person.

Hold each other accountable. The Live section is an important gear in the "redefinition" machine. If you're really ready for positive change—for spiritual growth—you'll want to take this section seriously. Get personal when you summarize your discoveries. Be practical as you compose your goals. And make sure you're realistic as you determine a plan for accountability. Be extraordinarily loving but brutally honest as you examine each other's Live sections. The stuff on this page must be doable. Don't hold back—this is where the rubber meets the road.

frequently asked questions

I'm stuck. I've read the words on the page, but they just don't connect. Am I missing something?
Be patient. There's no need for speed-reading. Reread the words. Pray about them. Reflect on the questions at the bottom of the page. Consider rewriting the reading in a way that makes sense to you. Meditate on one idea at a time. Read Scripture passages in different Bible translations. Ask a friend for help. Skip the section and come back to it later. And don't beat yourself up if you still don't connect. Turn the page and keep seeking.

This study includes a wide variety of readings. Some are intended to provoke. Others are intended to subdue. Some are meant to apply to a thinker, others to a feeler, and still others to an experiential learner. If your groove is pop culture, science, relationships, art, or something completely different, there's something in here that you're naturally going to click with, but that doesn't mean that you should just brush off the rest of the readings. It means that in those no-instant-click moments, you're going to have to broaden your perspective and think outside your own box. You may be surprised by what you discover.

One or two people in our small group tend to dominate the discussion. Is there any polite way of handling this?
Did you set up ground rules with your group? If not, review the suggestions in the previous section and incorporate them. Then do this: Before each discussion, remind participants that each person's thoughts, insights, concerns, and opinions are important. Note the time you have for your meeting and then dive in.

If this still doesn't help, you may need to speak to the person who has arm-wrestled control. Do so in a loving manner, expressing your sincere concern for what the person is talking about and inviting others to weigh in as well. Please note: A one-person-dominated discussion isn't *always* a bad thing. Your role in a small group is not only to explore and expand your own understanding; it's also to support one another. If someone truly needs more of the floor, give it to him. There will be times when the needs of the one outweigh the needs of the many. Use good judgment and allow extra space when needed. Your time might be next week.

One or two people in our small group rarely say anything. How should we handle this?
Recognize that not everyone will be comfortable sharing. Depending on her background, personality, and comfort level, an individual may rarely say anything at all. There are two things to remember. First, love a person right where she is. This may be one of her first experiences as part of a Bible discussion group. She may be feeling insecure because she doesn't know the Bible as well as other members of the group. She may just be shy or introverted. She may still be sorting out what she believes. Whatever the case, make her feel welcome and loved. Thank her for coming, and if she misses a meeting, call to check up on her. After one of the studies, you may want to ask her what she thought about the discussion. And after a few meetings, you can try to involve her in the discussion by asking everyone in the group to respond to a certain question. Just make sure the question you ask doesn't put anyone on the spot.

During our meeting time, we find ourselves spending so much time catching up with each other — what happened over the previous week — that we don't have enough time for the actual study.
If the friendships within your group grow tight, you may need to establish some time just to hang out and catch up with one another. This is a healthy part of a successful discussion group. You can do this before or after the actual study group time. Some groups prefer to share a meal together before the study, and other groups prefer to stay afterward and munch on snacks. Whatever your group chooses, it's important to have established start and finish times for your group members. That way, the people who are on a tight schedule can know when to show up to catch the main part of the meeting.

At our meetings, there are times when one or two people will become really vulnerable about something they're struggling with or facing. It's an awkward thing for our group to try to handle. What should we do?

This study is designed to encourage group members to get real and be vulnerable. But how your group deals with those vulnerabilities will determine how much deeper your group can go. If a person is sharing something that makes her particularly vulnerable, avoid offering a quick, fix-it answer. Even if you know how to heal deep hurts, cure eating disorders, or overcome depression in one quick answer, hold your tongue. Most people who make themselves vulnerable aren't looking for a quick fix. They want two things: to know they aren't alone and to be supported. If you can identify with their hurt, say so, without one-upping their story with your own. Second, let the person know you'll pray for her, and if the moment is right, go ahead and pray for her right then. If the moment isn't right, then you may want to pray for her at the end of the meeting. Walking through these vulnerable times is tricky business, and it's going to take a lot of prayer and listening to God's leading to get you through.

Some group members don't prepare before our meetings. How can we encourage them to read ahead of time?

It can be frustrating, particularly as a leader, when group members don't read the material; but don't let this discourage you. You can begin each lesson by reading the section together as a group so that everyone is on the same page. And you can gently encourage group members to read during the week. But ultimately, what really matters is that they show up and are growing spiritually alongside you. The REDEFINING LIFE studies aren't about homework; they're about personal spiritual growth, and that takes place in many ways—both inside and outside this book. So if someone's slacking on the outside, it's okay. You have no idea how much she may be growing or being challenged on the inside.

Our group members are having a tough time reaching their goals. What can we do?

First of all, review the goals you've set. Are they realistic? How would you measure a goal of "don't be frustrated at work"? Rewrite the goals until they're bite-sized and reasonable—and reachable. How about "Take an online personality test" or "Make a list of what's good and what's not-so-good about my career choices so I can talk about it with discussion group members" or "Start keeping a prayer journal." Get practical. Get real. And don't forget to marinate everything in lots of prayer.

notes

Lesson 1
1. Reprinted by permission. *Captivating*, John and Stasi Eldredge, 2005, Thomas Nelson Inc. Nashville, Tennessee, p. 4. All rights reserved.
2. Eldredge, pp. 6-7.
3. C. S. Lewis, "Modern Man and His Categories of Thought" in *Present Concerns: A Compelling Collection of Timely, Journalistic Essays*, ed. Walter Hooper (New York: Harcourt Brace Jovanovich, 1986), pp. 62-63.

Lesson 2
1. A.W. Tozer, *The Pursuit of God* (Camp Hill, Pa.: Christian Publications, 1993), pp. 96-97.
2. Rob Bell, *Velvet Elvis* (Grand Rapids, Mich.: Zondervan, 2005), pp. 34-35. Used by permission of The Zondervan Corporation.
3. Donald Miller, *Searching for God Knows What* (Nashville: Nelson, 2004), p. 116.

Lesson 3
1. Abby Wilner, "Q & A: Zach Braff: *Scrubs* Star Branches Out in Directorial Debut of *Garden State*," http://www.hatchmagazine.com/story.phtml?id=197.
2. Margaret Feinberg, *What the Heck Am I Going to Do with My Life? Find Your Place in This World* (Chicago: Tyndale, forthcoming).
3. Alexandra Robbins and Abby Wilner, *Quarterlife Crisis: The Unique Challenges of Life in Your Twenties* (New York: Tarcher, 2001), pp. 112-113. Used by permission of Jeremy P. Tarcher, an imprint of Penguin Group (USA) Inc.

Lesson 4
1. Bill Saxman, "Friendship," October 12, 2002, http://www.theooze.com/articles/article.cfm?id=351&page=1.
2. Jane Rubietta, "Soul Sisters," *LifeWay*, http://www.lifeway.com/lwc/article_main_page/0%2C1703%2CA%253D158014%2526M%253D200391%2C00.html.

3. Annette Smith, "Tell It Like It Is: How to Speak the Truth to a Friend Without Harming Your Friendship," *Today's Christian Woman*, November/December 2002, http://www.christianitytoday.com/tcw/2002/006/9.86.html. Published by Christianity Today International, Carol Stream, Illinois.

Lesson 5
1. Les and Leslie Parrott, "Can Men and Women Be Just Friends?," *Christianity Today*, December 2002, http://www.christianitytoday.com/singles/eharmony/02dec-6.html.
2. Gene Edward Veith, "Sexual Healing," *WORLD* magazine, May 7, 2005, http://www.worldmag.com/subscriber/displayarticle.cfm?id=10601. Used by permission © 2005 WORLD magazine, all rights reserved.

Lesson 6
1. Carin Gorrell, "Finding Fault," *Psychology Today*, September/October 2001, http://www.psychologytoday.com/articles/pto-20010901-000014.html. Reprinted with permission from *Psychology Today* magazine, Copyright © (2001) Sussex Publishers, Inc.
2. Reprinted from Constance Rhodes, *Life Inside the "Thin" Cage: A Personal Look into the Hidden World of the Chronic Dieter,* pp. 5-6. Used by permission of WaterBrook Press, Colorado Springs, CO. All rights reserved.
3. Lisa Collier Cool, "Are You Addicted to Stress?," *Redbook*, July 2005, p. 172.

Lesson 7
1. T. M. Moore, *Disciplines of Grace: From Spiritual Routines to Spiritual Renewal* (Downers Grove, Ill.: InterVarsity, 2001), p. 16.
2. Margaret Feinberg, "Learning to Exhale: Embrace the Gift of True Sabbath Rest and Gain a New Outlook on Life," *Home Life*, August 2005, p. 49.
3. Gary L. Thomas, *Authentic Faith: The Power of a Fire-Tested Life* (Grand Rapids, Mich.: Zondervan, 2002), pp. 50-51. Used by permission of The Zondervan Corporation.

Lesson 8
1. Brian Orme, "Ruined," *Relevant*, n.d., http://www.relevantmagazine.com/god_article.php?id=7014.
2. Jerusha Clark, *Every Thought Captive: Battling the Toxic Beliefs That Separate Us from the Life We Crave* (Colorado Springs, Colo.: TH1NK, 2006), pp. 14-15.
3. Joyce Meyer, *Battlefield of the Mind: Winning the Battle in Your Mind* (New York: Warner Faith, 2002), p. 69.

DEFINE YOUR LIFE BY GOD'S WORD.

Redefining Life: My Relationships
TH1NK
1-57683-888-9
Learn how you can be a better friend, roommate, or girlfriend with this practical, advice-filled study.

Redefining Life: My Purpose
TH1NK
1-57683-827-7
In this discussion guide, you will be challenged to ask yourself some tough questions about your significance and where you find it.

Redefining Life: My Identity
TH1NK
1-57683-828-5
There is freedom in knowing who you are. With this discussion guide, you'll not only discover what you were created for but also learn about the One who created you.

Redefining Life: My Career
TH1NK
1-57683-887-0
This study helps you navigate through tough job interviews, survive office politics, understand cubicle etiquette, and find out how to represent Christ in your new environment.

Visit your local Christian bookstore, call NavPress at 1-800-366-7788, or log on to www.navpress.com to purchase.

To locate a Christian bookstore near you, call 1-800-991-7747.